EYEWIT...
PHRASE BOOK
SPANISH

D0819125

DK

REVISED EDITION

DK LONDON

Senior Editor Christine Stroyan
Senior Art Editors Anna Hall, Amy Child
Art Director Karen Self
Associate Publisher Liz Wheeler
Publishing Director Jonathan Metcalf
Proofreading Elena Ureña, in association with
First Edition Translations Ltd, Cambridge, UK
Senior Pre-Producer Andy Hilliard
Senior Producers Gary Batchelor, Anna Vallarino

DK DELHI

Assistant Editor Sugandha Agarwal
Assistant Art Editors
Anukriti Arora, Devika Khosla,
Art Editors Ravi Indiver, Mansi Agarwal
Senior Art Editor Chhaya Sajwan
Managing Editor Soma B. Chowdhury
Senior Managing Art Editor
Arunesh Talapatra

Production Manager Pankaj Sharma
Preproduction Managers
Sunil Sharma, Balwant Singh
Senior DTP Designers
Tarun Sharma, Jaypal Singh,
Neeraj Bhatia, Ajay Verma

First American edition 2008
This revised edition published in 2017 by
DK Publishing,
345 Hudson Street, New York, New York 10014

Copyright © 2008, 2017 Dorling Kindersley Limited
DK, a Division of Penguin Random House LLC
17 18 19 20 10 9 8 7 6 5 4 3 2 1
001–300210–Jun/2017

A catalog record for this book is available from the Library of Congress.
ISBN: 978-1-4654-6281-7

Printed and bound in China

A WORLD OF IDEAS:
SEE ALL THERE IS TO KNOW

www.dk.com

CONTENTS

INTRODUCTION

This book provides all the key words and phrases you are likely to need in everyday situations. It is grouped into themes, and key phrases are broken down into short sections, to help you build a wide variety of sentences. A lot of the vocabulary is illustrated to make it easy to remember, and "You may hear" boxes feature questions you are likely to hear. At the back of the book there is a menu guide, listing about 500 food terms, and a 2,000-word two-way dictionary.

NOUNS

All Spanish nouns (words for things, people, and ideas) are masculine or feminine. The gender of nouns is shown by the word used for "the": **el** (generally masculine singular, but sometimes feminine; see the Spanish–English dictionary on pp195–222), **la** (feminine singular), **los** (masculine plural), or **las** (feminine plural).

ADJECTIVES

Most Spanish adjectives change endings according to whether they describe a masculine or feminine, singular or plural word. In this book the singular masculine form is shown, followed by the alternative feminine ending:

I'm married   **Soy casado/a.**

"YOU"

There are two ways of saying "you" in Spanish: **usted** (polite) and **tú** (familiar). In this book we have used **usted**, as it is normally used with people you don't know.

VERBS

Verbs usually change depending on whether they are in the singular or plural. Where this happens, you will see the singular form of the verb followed by the plural form:

Where is/are...?   **¿Dónde está/están...?**

PRONUNCIATION GUIDE

Below each Spanish word or phrase in this book, you will find a pronunciation guide. Read it as if it were English and you should be understood, but remember that it is only a guide and for the best results you should listen to the native speakers in the audio app and try to mimic them. Some Spanish sounds are different from those in English and this book teaches European Spanish (Castilian), which differs in pronunciation from Latin American Spanish. Take note of how the letters below are pronounced.

a	like "a" in "cap"
c	before "a," "o," and "u," like "k" in "kite" before "i" and "e," like "th" in "thin"
e	like "e" in "wet" at the end of a word, like "ay" in "may"
g	before "a," "o," and "u," like "g" in "got" before "e" and "i," like "ch" in the Scottish word "loch"
h	silent
i	like "ee" in "keep"
ie	in the middle of a word, like "y" in "yes"
j	like "ch" in the Scottish word "loch"
ll	like "y" in "yes"
ñ	like "ni" in "onion"
o	like "oa" in "boat"
q	like "k" in "king"
r	trilled like a Scottish "r," especially at the beginning of a word and when double "r"
u	like "oo" in "boot"
v	like a soft "b"
z	like "th" in "thin"

FREE EYEWITNESS TRAVEL
PHRASE BOOK AUDIO APP

The audio app that accompanies this phrase book contains nearly 1,000 essential Spanish words and phrases, spoken by native speakers, for use when traveling or when preparing for your trip.

HOW TO USE THE AUDIO APP

- Download the free app on your smartphone or tablet from the App Store or Google Play.
- Open the app and scan or key in the barcode on the back of your Eyewitness Phrase Book to add the book to your Library.
- Download the audio files for your language.
- The 🎧 symbol in the book indicates that there is audio for that section. Enter the page number from the book into the search field in the app to bring up the list of words and phrases for that page or section. You can then scroll up and down through the list to find the word or phrase you want.
- Tap a word or phrase to hear it.
- Swipe left or right to view the previous or next page.
- Add phrases you will use often to your Favorites.

ESSENTIALS

In this section, you will find the essential words and useful phrases that you will need in Spain for basic everyday talk and situations. You should be aware of cultural differences when you are addressing Spanish people and remember that they tend to be quite formal with strangers, often using the polite *usted* form of address, rather than the more familiar *tú* for "you" and shaking hands. Use the formal form with people you don't know.

GREETINGS

Hello
Hola
ohlah

Good evening
Buenas tardes
bwenas tardais

Good night
Buenas noches
bwenas nochais

Goodbye
Adiós
adyos

Hi/bye!
¡Hola/adiós!
ohlah/adyos

Pleased to meet you
Encantado de conocerle
enkantadoh day konotherlay

How are you?
¿Cómo está?
komoh estah

Fine, thanks
Bien, gracias
byen grathyas

You're welcome
De nada
day nadah

My name is...
Me llamo...
may yamoh

What's your name?
¿Cómo se llama?
komoh say yamah

What's his/her name?
¿Cómo se llama él/ella?
komoh say yamah el/eyah

This is...
Éste es...
estay es

Nice to meet you
Mucho gusto
moochoh goostoh

See you tomorrow
Hasta mañana
astah manyanah

See you soon
Hasta pronto
astah prontoh

SMALL TALK

Yes/no	Sí/no *see/noh*
Please	Por favor *por fabor*
Thank you (very much)	(Muchas) gracias *moochas grathyas*
You're welcome	De nada *day nadah*
OK/fine	Bien *byen*
Pardon?	¿Perdón? *pairdon*
Excuse me	Disculpe *deeskoolpay*
Sorry	Lo siento *loh syentoh*
I don't know	No lo sé *noh loh say*
I don't understand	No le entiendo *noh lay aintyendoh*
Could you repeat that?	¿Puede repetir? *pweday repeteer*
I don't speak Spanish	No hablo español *noh ahbloh espanyol*
Do you speak English?	¿Habla usted inglés? *ahblah oosted eenglais*
What is the Spanish for...?	¿Cómo se dice...en español? *komoh say deethay...en espanyol*
What's that called?	¿Cómo se llama eso? *komoh say yamah esoh*
Can you tell me...	¿Puede decirme...? *pweday detheermay*

TALKING ABOUT YOURSELF

I'm from...	Soy de... *soy day*
I'm...	Soy... *soy*
...American	...estadounidense *...aistadoh-oonydensay*
...English	...inglés/inglesa *...eenglais/eenglaisah*
...Canadian	...canadiense *...kanadyensay*
...Australian	...australiano/a *...noostralyanoh/ah*
...single	...soltero/a *...solteroh/ah*
...married	...casado/a *...kasadoh/ah*
...divorced	...divorciado/a *...deehorthyadoh/ah*
I am...years old	Tengo...años *taingoh...anyos*
I have...	Tengo... *taingoh*
...a boyfriend/girlfriend	...novio/novia *...nobyo/nobya*
...two children	...dos hijos *...dos eehos*
Where are you from?	¿De dónde es usted? *day donday es oosted*
Are you married?	¿Está casado? *estah kasadoh*
Do you have children?	¿Tiene hijos? *tyenay eehos*

SOCIALIZING

Do you live here?   ¿Vive aquí?
beebay ahkee

Where do you live?   ¿Dónde vive?
donday beebay

I am here...   Estoy aquí...
estoy ahkee

...on vacation   ...de vacaciones
day bakathyonais

...on business   ...en viaje de negocios
en beeyahay day negothyos

I'm a student   Soy estudiante
soy estoodyantay

I work in...   Trabajo en...
trabahoh en

I am retired   Estoy jubilado
estoy hoobeeladoh

Can I have...   ¿Me da...
may dah

...your telephone number?   ...su número de teléfono?
soo noomeroh day telefonoh

...your email address?   ...su dirección de email?
soo deerekthyon day eemaeel

It doesn't matter   No importa
noh eemportah

Cheers!   Salud
salood

I don't drink/smoke   No bebo alcohol/no fumo
noh beboh alkol/noh foomoh

Are you alright?   ¿Se encuentra bien?
say enkwentrah byen

I'm OK   Estoy bien
estoy byen

LIKES AND DISLIKES

I like/love...

Me gusta/encanta...
may goostah/enkantah

I don't like...

No me gusta...
noh may goostah

I hate...

Detesto...
daytestoh

I rather/really like...

Me gusta bastante/mucho...
may goostah bastantuy/moochoh

Don't you like it?

¿No te gusta?
noh tay goostah

I would like...

Quisiera...
keesyerah

I'd like this one/that one

Quisiera éste/ése
keesyerah estay/esay

My favorite is .

Mi preferido es...
mee prefereedoh es

I prefer...

Prefiero...
prefyeroh

It's delicious

Está delicioso
estah dayleethyosoh

What would you like
to do?

¿Qué le gustaría hacer?
kay lay goostarya ahthair

I don't mind

Me da igual
may dah ygwal

Do you like...?

¿Le gusta...?
lay goostah

YOU MAY HEAR...

¿Qué hace?
kay ahthay
What do you do?

¿Está de vacaciones?
estah day bakathyonais
Are you on vacation?

DAYS OF THE WEEK

What day is it today?	¿Qué día es hoy? *kay deeyah es oi*	Friday	viernes *byernais*
Sunday	domingo *domeengoh*	Saturday	sábado *sabadoh*
Monday	lunes *loonais*	today	hoy *oi*
Tuesday	martes *martais*	tomorrow	mañana *manyanah*
Wednesday	miércoles *myerkolais*	yesterday	ayer *ayair*
Thursday	jueves *hooebes*	in...days	dentro de...días *daintro day...deeyas*

THE SEASONS

primavera
preemabairah
spring

verano
bairanoh
summer

MONTHS

January	enero *aineroh*	July	julio *hoolyoh*
February	febrero *febrairoh*	August	agosto *agostoh*
March	marzo *marthoh*	September	septiembre *saiptyembray*
April	abril *ahbreel*	October	octubre *oktoobray*
May	mayo *mayoh*	November	noviembre *nobyembray*
June	junio *hoonyoh*	December	diciembre *deethyembray*

otoño
otonyoh
fall

invierno
eenbyernoh
winter

TELLING THE TIME

What time is it?	¿Qué hora es? *kay ohrah es*
It's nine o'clock	Son las nueve *son las nwaibay*
...in the morning	...de la mañana *day lah manyanah*
...in the afternoon	...de la tarde *day lah tarday*
...in the evening	...de la noche *day lah nochay*

la una en punto
lah oonah en poontoh
one o'clock

la una y diez
lah oonah ee deeyaith
ten past one

la una y cuarto
lah oonah ee kwartoh
quarter past one

la una y veinte
lah oonah ee baintay
twenty past one

la una y media
lah oonah ee medya
half past one

la dos menos cuarto
las dos mainos kwartoh
quarter to two

las dos menos diez
las dos mainos deeyaith
ten to two

las dos en punto
las dos en poontoh
two o'clock

It's noon/midnight	Es mediodía/medianoche
	es meeyodeeyah/medyanochay
second	el segundo
	el saigoondoh
minute	el minuto
	el meenootoh
hour	la hora
	lah ohrah
a quarter of an hour	un cuarto de hora
	oon kwartoh day ohrah
half an hour	media hora
	maiya ohrah
three-quarters of an hour	tres cuartos de hora
	trais kwartos day ohrah
late	tarde
	tarday
early	temprano
	taimpranoh
soon	pronto
	prontoh
What time does it start?	¿A qué hora empieza?
	ah kay ohrah empyethah
What time does it finish?	¿A qué hora termina?
	ah kay ohrah termeenah

YOU MAY HEAR...

Hasta luego	Llega temprano	Llega tarde
astah lwegoh	*yegah taimpranoh*	*yegah tarday*
See you later	**You're early**	**You're late**

THE WEATHER

What's the forecast?	¿Cuál es la previsión del tiempo? *kwal es lah praibeesyon dail tyempoh*
What's the weather like?	¿Qué tiempo hace? *kay tyempoh ahthay*
It's...	Hace... *ahthay*
...good	...bueno *bwenoh*
...bad	...mal tiempo *mal tyempoh*
...warm	...una buena temperatura *oonah bwenah temperatoorah*
...hot	...calor *kalor*
...cold	...frío *freeyoh*

Hace sol
ahthay sol
It's sunny

Está
lloviendo
*estah
yobyendoh*
It's raining

Está nublado
*estah
noobladoh*
It's cloudy

Hay
tormenta
*ah-ee
tormaintah*
It's stormy

What's the temperature?	¿Qué temperatura hace? *kay temperatoorah ahthay*
It's...degrees	...grados *grahdos*
It's a beautiful day	Hace un día precioso *ahthay oon deeyah prethyosoh*
The weather's changing	El tiempo está cambiando *el tyempoh estah kambyandoh*
Is it going to get colder/hotter?	¿Empezará a hacer más frío/calor? *empetharah ah ahthair mas freeyoh/kalor*
It's cooling down	Hace más frío *ahthay mas freeyoh*
Is it going to freeze?	¿Helará? *ehlahrah*

Está nevando
estah naibandoh
It's snowing

Hay hielo
ah-ee yeloh
It's icy

Hay niebla
ah-ee nyeblah
It's misty

Hace viento
ahthay byentoh
It's windy

GETTING AROUND

Spain has a good road and highway network
if you are traveling around the country by car. Spanish
trains are fast and punctual, linking the major towns
and cities. The high-speed AVE service links the capital
Madrid with Seville in the south. You can also travel,
of course, by taxi, bus, coach, or plane. In the cities of
Madrid, Barcelona and Bilbao, the *Metro* (subway) is a
quick and easy way of getting around.

ASKING WHERE THINGS ARE

Excuse me, please | Disculpe, por favor
deeskoolpay por fabor

Where is... | ¿Dónde está...
donday estah

...the town center? | ...el centro?
el thentroh

...the train station? | ...la estación de tren?
lah estathyon dey tren

...the cash machine? | ...el cajero automático?
el kaheroh ah-ootomateekoh

How do I get to...? | ¿Cómo se va a...?
komon say bah ah

I'm going to... | Voy a...
Boy ah

I'm looking for... | Busco...
booskoh

I'm lost | Me he perdido
may perdeedoh

Is it near? | ¿Está cerca?
estah therkah

Is there a...nearby? | ¿Hay un...por aquí cerca?
ah-ee oon...por ahkee therkah

Is it far? | ¿Está lejos?
estah lehos

How far is... | ¿Queda muy lejos...
kedah mooy lehos

...the town hall? | ...el ayuntamiento?
el ayoontamyentoh

...the market? | ...el mercado?
el merkadoh

Can I walk there? | ¿Se puede ir andando?
say pweday eer andandoh

CAR AND BIKE RENTAL

Where is the car rental desk?	¿Dónde está el mostrador de alquiler de coches? *donday estah el mostrador day alkeelair day kochais*
I want to rent...	Quiero alquilar... *kyero alkeelar*
...a car	...un coche *oon kochay*
...a bicycle	...una bicicleta *oonah beetheekletah*
for...days	para...días *parah...deeyas*
for a week	para una semana *parah oonah semanah*

el turismo
el tooreesmoh
sedan

el coche de cinco puertas
el kochay day theenkoh pwertas
hatchback

la moto
lah moto
motorcycle

la vespa
lah baispah
scooter

la bicicleta de montaña
lah beetheekletah day montanyah
mountain bike

for the weekend	para el fin de semana *parah el feen day semanah*
I'd like...	Lo quisiera... *loh keesyerah*
...an automatic	...automático *ah-ootomateekoh*
...a manual	...manual *manooal*
Has it got air-conditioning?	¿Tiene aire acondicionado? *tyenay ah-yray ahkondeethyonadoh*
Should I return it with a full tank?	¿Tengo que devolverlo con el depósito lleno? *taingoh kay debolberloh kon el daiposeetoh yenoh*
Here's my driver's license	Aquí tiene mi carné de conducir *ahkee tyenay mee karneh day kondootheer*
Can I rent a GPS receiver...?	¿Puedo alquilar un GPS? *pwedoh alkeelar oon hay puy esay*

el casco de ciclismo
el kaskoh day theekleesmoh
cycling helmet

el candado
el kandadoh
lock

la mancha
lah manchah
pump

la silla para niños
lah seeyah parah neenyos
child seat

DRIVING

Is this the road to...?	¿Es ésta la carretera que lleva a...? *es estah lah karreterah kay yebah ah*
Where is the nearest garage?	¿Dónde está el garaje más cercano? *donday estah el garahay mas therkanoh*
I'd like...	Póngame... *pongamay*
...some gas	...gasolina *gasoleenah*
...40 liters of unleaded	...cuarenta litros de gasolina sin plomo *kwahrentah lee-tros day gasoleenah seen plomoh*
...30 liters of diesel	...treinta litros de diésel *traintah lee-tros day deeyaysail*
Fill it up, please	Lleno, por favor *yenoh por fabor*
Where do I pay?	¿Dónde hay que pagar? *donday ah-y kay pagar*
The pump number is...	El número del surtidor es... *el noomeroh dail soorteedor es*
Can I pay by credit card?	¿Se puede pagar con tarjeta de crédito? *say pweday pagar kon tarhetah day kredeetoh*
Please, would you check...	Por favor, compruebe... *por fabor komprwebay*
...the oil	...el aceite *el ahthaytay*
...the tire pressure	...la presión de las ruedas *lah presyon day las rwedas*

PARKING

Is there a parking lot nearby?	¿Hay un aparcamiento por aquí cerca? *ah-ee oon ahparkamyentoh por ahkee therkah*
Can I park here?	¿Se puede aparcar aquí? *say pweday ahparkar ahkee*
How long can I park for?	¿Cuánto tiempo se puede aparcar? *kwanto tyempoh say pweday ahparkar*
How much does it cost?	¿Cuánto cuesta? *kwanto kwestah*
How much is it...	¿Cuánto es... *kwanto es*
...per hour?	...por hora? *por ohrah*
...per day?	...por día? *por deeyuh*
...overnight?	...por toda la noche? *por todah lah nochay*

la silla infantil
para el coche
*lah seeyah
eenfanteel parah
el kochay*
child seat

la gasolinera
lah gasoleenerah
gas station

THE CAR

el maletero
el maleteroh
trunk

el tubo de escape
el tooboh day eskapay
exhaust

la rueda
lah rwedah
wheel

la puerta
lah pwertah
door

INSIDE THE CAR

el asiento delantero
el ahsyaintoh dailanteroh
front seat

el cierre de la puerta
el thyerray day lah pwertah
door lock

el cinturón de seguridad
el theentooron day segooreedad
seat belt

el asiento trasero
el ahsyentoh traseroh
back seat

el parabrisas
el parabreesa
windshield

el capó
el kapoh
hood

el faro
el faroh
headlight

el parachoques
el parachokais
bumper

el neumático
el ne-oomateekoh
tire

el motor
el motor
engine

THE CONTROLS

el equipo
estéreo del coche
el ekeepoh estereoh del kochay
car stereo

las luces de emergencia
*lahs loothais day
emerhenthya*
hazard lights

el velocímetro
el belotheemetroh
speedometer

el airbag
el ahyeerbag
air bag

el salpicadero
el salpeekaderoh
dashboard

la calefacción
*lah
kalefakthyon*
heater

el cláxon
el klakson
horn

la palanca de
cambios
*lah palankah
day kambyos*
gear shift

el volante
el bolantay
steering wheel

ROAD SIGNS

sentido obligatorio
senteedo ohbleegatoryoh
one way

glorieta
gloryetah
traffic circle

ceda el paso
thedah el pasoh
yield

entrada prohibida
entradah proybeedah
no entry

calzada con prioridad
*kalthadah kon
pryoreedad*
priority road

**estacionamiento
prohibido**
*estathyonamyentoh
proybeedoh*
no parking

velocidad máxima
belotheedad makseemah
speed limit

peligro
peleegroh
hazard

ON THE ROAD

el parquímetro
el parkeemetroh
parking meter

el semáforo
el saimaforoh
traffic light

el guardia de tráfico
el gwardyah day trafeekoh
traffic police officer

el paso de peatones
el pahsoh day peahtonais
pedestrian crossing

el mapa
el mapah
map

**el aparcamiento
para minusválidos**
*el ahparkamyentoh
parah meenoosbaleedos*
disabled parking

la autopista
lah ahootopeestah
highway

la vía de acceso
lah bee-ah day akthesoh
entrance/exit ramp

**el teléfono de
emergencias**
*el telefonoh day
aimerhenthyas*
emergency phone

AT THE STATION 🎧

Where can I buy a ticket?	¿Dónde se puede comprar un billete? *donday say pweday komprar oon beeyetay*
Is there an automatic ticket machine?	¿Hay una máquina de billetes? *ah-ee oonah makeenah day beeyetais*
How much is a ticket to...?	¿Cuánto cuesta un billete para...? *kwantoh kwestah oon beeyetay parah*
Two tickets to...	Dos billetes para... *dos beeyetais parah*
I'd like...	Quisiera... *keesyerah*
...a one-way ticket to...	...un billete de ida para... *oon beeyetay day eedah parah*
...a return ticket to...	...un billete de ida y vuelta para... *oon beeyetay day eedah ee bweltah parah*
...a first-class ticket	...un billete de clase preferente *oon beeyetay day klasay praiferentay*
...a standard-class ticket	...un billete de clase turista *oon beeyetay day klasay tooreestah*

la máquina expendedora de billetes
lah makeenah ekspendedorah day beeyetais
automatic ticket machine

I'd like to...	Quisiera... *keesyerah*
...reserve a seat	...reservar un asiento *reserbar oon ahsyentoh*
...on the AVE/TALGO to...	...en el AVE/TALGO para... *en el ahbay/talgoh parah*
...book a sleeper berth	...reservar una litera *reserbar oonuh leeterah*
Is there a reduction...?	¿Hay descuentos... *ah-ee daiskwentos*
...for children?	...para niños? *parah neenyos*
...for students?	...para estudiantes? *parah estoodyantais*
...for senior citizens?	...para la tercera edad? *parah lah tertherah edad*
Is there a dining car?	¿Hay vagón restaurante? *ah-ee bagon raista-oorantay*
Is it a high-speed train?	¿Es un tren de alta velocidad? *es oon tren day altah belotheedad*
Is it a fast/slow train?	¿Es un tren rápido/lento? *es oon tren rapeedoh/lentoh*

YOU MAY HEAR...

El tren sale de la vía número...
el tren salay day lah beeyah noomeroh
The train leaves from platform...

Deberá hacer trasbordo en...
deberah ahthair trasbordoh
You must change trains at...

TRAVELING BY TRAIN 🎧

Do you have a timetable?	¿Tiene un horario? *Tyenay oon ohraryoh*
What time is...	¿A qué hora sale... *ah kay ohrah salay*
...the next train to...?	...el próximo tren para...? *el prokseemoh tren parah*
...the last train to...?	...el último tren para...? *el oolteemoh tren parah*
Which platform does it leave from?	¿De qué vía sale? *day kay beeyah salay*
What time does it arrive in...?	¿A qué hora llega a...? *ah kay ohrah yegah ah*
How long does it take?	¿Cuánto tarda? *kwantoh tardah*
Is this the train for...?	¿Es éste el tren para...? *es estay el tren parah*
Is this the right platform for...?	¿Es ésta la vía del tren para...? *es estah lah beeyah dayl tren parah*
Where is platform three?	¿Dónde está la vía tres? *donday estah lah beeyah trais*

YOU MAY HEAR...

¿Ha comprado el billete por Internet?
ah kompradoh el beeyetay por internet
Did you book online?

Tiene que imprimirlo en la máquina
tyenay kay eempreemeerloh en lah makeenah
Go to the collection point

Does this train stop at...?	¿Este tren para en...? *estay tren parah en*
Where do I change for...?	¿Dónde tengo que hacer trasbordo para...? *donday taingoh kay ahthair trasbordoh parah*
Is this seat free?	¿Está ocupado este asiento? *estah okoopadoh estay ahsyentoh*
I've reserved this seat	Tengo reservado este asiento *taingoh reserbadoh estay ahsyentoh*
Do I get off here?	¿Tengo que bajarme aquí? *taingoh kay baharmay ahkee*
Where is the subway station?	¿Dónde está la boca de metro? *donday estah lah bokah day metroh*
Which line goes to...?	¿Qué línea va a...? *kay leenay-uh bah ah*

la sala de la estación
lah salah day lah estathyon
concourse

el tren
el tren
train

el vagón comedor
el bagon komedor
dining car

la litera
lah leeterah
sleeper berth

BUSES

When is the next bus to...?	¿Cuándo sale el próximo autobús para...? *kwandoh salay el prokseemoh ah-ootoboos parah*
What is the fare to...?	¿Cuál es la tarifa para...? *kwal es lah tareefah parah*
Where is the nearest bus stop?	¿Dónde está la parada más próxima? *donday estah lah paradah mas prokseemah*
Is this the bus stop for...	¿Es ésta la parada de...? *es estah las paradah day*
Does the number 4 stop here?	¿Para aquí el autobús número 4? *parah ahkee el ah-ootoboos noomeroh kwatroh*
Where can I buy a ticket?	¿Dónde se puede comprar un billete? *donday say pweday komprar oon beeyetay*
Can I pay on the bus?	¿Se puede pagar en el autobús? *say pweday pagar en el ah-ootoboos*
Which buses go to the city center?	¿Qué autobuses van al centro? *kay ah-ootoboosays ban al thentroh*
I want to get off!	¡Quiero apearme! *kyeroh ahpai-armay*

la estación de autobuses
lah estathyon day ah-ootoboosays
bus station

TAXIS

Where can I get a taxi?	¿Dónde se puede coger un taxi? *donday say pweday kohair oon taksi*
Can I order a taxi?	¿Puedo pedir un taxi? *pwedoh paideer oon taksi*
I want a taxi to...	Quisiera un taxi para ir a... *keesyerah oon taksi parah eer ah*
Can you take me to...	Lléveme a... *yebemeh ah*
Is it far?	¿Está lejos? *estah lehos*
How much will it cost?	¿Cuánto cuesta? *kwantoh kwestah*
Can you drop me here?	¿Puede parar aquí? *pweday parar ahkee*
What do I owe you?	¿Cuánto le debo? *kwantoh lay deboh*
I don't have any change	¿Tiene cambio? *tyenay kambyo*
Keep the change	Quédese con el cambio *kedesay kon el kambyo*
May I have a receipt, please?	¿Puede darme un recibo? *pweday darmay oon retheeboh*
Please wait for me	Espéreme, por favor *esperemay por fabor*

el taxi
el taksi
taxi

BOATS

Are there any boat trips?	¿Hay excursiones en barco?
	ah-ee ekskoorsyonais en barkoh
Where does the boat leave from?	¿De dónde sale el barco?
	day donday salay el barkoh
When is...	¿Cuándo sale...
	kwandoh salay
...the next boat to...?	...el próximo barco para...?
	el prokseemoh barkoh parah
...the first boat?	...el primer barco?
	el preemair barkoh
...the last boat?	...el último barco?
	el oolteemoh barkoh
I'd like two tickets for...	Quisiera dos billetes para...
	keesyerah dos beeyetais parah
...the cruise	...el crucero
	el krootheroh

el ferry
el ferry
ferry

el aliscafo
el ahleeskafoh
hydrofoil

el yate
el yatay
yacht

el aerodeslizador
el ahairodesleethador
hovercraft

...the river trip ...la excursión por el río
lah ekskoorsyon por el reeo

How much is it for... ¿Cuánto cuesta...
kwantoh kwestah

...a car and two people? ...un coche y dos personas?
oon kochay ee dos personas

...a family? ...una familia?
oonah fameelya

...a cabin? ...un camarote?
oon kahmahrohtay

Can I buy a ticket ¿Se puede comprar el billete a bordo?
on board? *say pweday komprar el beeyetay ah bordoh*

Is there wheelchair ¿Dispone de acceso para sillas de
access? ruedas?
*deesponay day akthaisoh parah seeyas
day rwedas*

el barco
de recreo
*el barkoh
day raikreoh*
pleasure boat

el salvavidas
el salbabeedas
life ring

el catamarán
el katamaran
catamaran

el chaleco
salvavidas
*el chalekoh
salbabeedas*
life jacket

AIR TRAVEL

Which terminal do I need?	¿A qué terminal tengo que ir? *ah kay termeenal taingoh kay eer*
Where do I check in?	¿Dónde hay que facturar? *donday ah-y kay faktoorar*
Where is...	¿Dónde está... *donday estah*
...the arrivals hall?	...el vestíbulo de llegadas? *el besteebooloh day yegadas*
...the departures hall?	...el vestíbulo de salidas? *el besteebooloh day saleedas*
...the boarding gate?	...la puerta de embarque? *lah pwertah day embarkay*
I'm traveling...	Viajo en... *beeyahoh en*
...economy	...clase turista *klasay tooreestah*
...business class	...clase preferente *klasay praiferentay*

la bolsa de viaje
lah bolsah day beeyahay
duffel bag

el pasaporte
el pasaportay
passport

la comida de avión
lah komeedah day ahbyon
in-flight meal

la tarjeta de embarque
lah tarhetah day embarkay
boarding pass

I'm checking in one suitcase

Facturo una maleta
faktooroh oonah maletah

I packed it myself

Yo mismo he hecho la maleta
yoh meesmoh eh echoh lah maletah

I have one piece of hand luggage

Llevo equipaje de mano
yeboh ekeepahay day manoh

How much is excess baggage?

¿Cuánto hay que pagar por exceso de equipaje?
kwantoh ah-ee kay pagar por eksthesoh day ekeepahay

Will a meal be served?

¿Se servirá alguna comida?
se serbeerah algoonah komeedah

I'd like...

Quisiera...
keesyerah

...a window seat

...un asiento de ventanilla
oon asyentoh day bentaneeyah

...an aisle seat

...un asiento de pasillo
oon asyentoh day paseeyoh

...a bulk head seat

...un asiento de mamparo
oon asyentoh day mamparoh

YOU MAY HEAR...

Su pasaporte/billete, por favor
soo pasaportay/beeyetay por fabor
Your passport/ticket, please

¿Es éste su bolso?
es estay soo bolsoh
Is this your bag?

AT THE AIRPORT

Here's my...
Aquí tiene...
ahkee tyenay

...boarding pass
...mi tarjeta de embarque
mee tarhetah day embarkay

...passport
...mi pasaporte
mee pasaportay

Can I change some money?
¿Puedo cambiar dinero?
pwedoh kambyar deeneroh

What is the exchange rate?
¿A cuánto está el cambio?
ah kwanatoh estah el kambyo

Is the flight delayed?
¿El vuelo llega con retraso?
el bweloh yegah kon raitrasoh

Oficina de cambio de divisas
ohfeeceenah de kambyo day deebeesas
currency exchange booth

el control de pasaportes
el kontrol day pasaportais
passport control

la tienda libre de impuestos
lah tyendah leebray day eempwestos
duty-free shop

la recogida de equipajes
lah rekoheedah day ekeepahais
baggage claim

el avión
el ahbyon
airplane

la azafata
lah athafatah
flight attendant

How late is it?	¿Tiene mucho retraso? *tyenay moochoh raitrasoh*
Which gate does flight... leave from?	¿De qué puerta sale el vuelo...? *day kay pwertah salay el bweloh*
What time do I board?	¿A qué hora tengo que embarcar? *ah kay ohrah tengoh kay embarkar*
When does the gate close?	¿Cuándo cierra la puerta de embarque? *kwandoh thyerah lah pwertah day embarkay*
Where are the carts?	¿Dónde están los carritos? *donday estan los kareetos*
Here is the baggage claim tag	Ésta es la etiqueta de identificación de equipaje *estah es lah eteeketah day eedenteefeekathyon day ekeepahay*
I can't find my baggage	No encuentro mi equipaje *noh enkwentroh mee ekeepahay*

EATING OUT

It is not difficult to eat well and inexpensively in Spain. You can choose from cafés and bars, which serve a range of drinks and hot and cold snacks (*tapas*), as well as family-run restaurants offering regional dishes, and more formal establishments. After a light breakfast, the Spanish tend to eat a substantial lunch between 2 p.m. and 3 p.m. followed by a *siesta*, and most do not eat their evening meal until after 10 p.m. – very late by some standards.

MAKING A RESERVATION

I'd like to book a table...
Quisiera reservar una mesa...
keesyerah reserbar oonah mesah

...for lunch/dinner
...para comer/cenar
parah komair/thenar

...for four people
...para cuatro personas
parah kwatroh personas

...for this evening
...para esta noche
parah estah nochay

...for tomorrow at one
...para mañana a la una
parah manyanah ah lah oonah

...for lunchtime today
...para hoy al mediodía
parah oi al medyodeeya

Do you have a table earlier/later?
¿Tiene una mesa más temprano/tarde?
tyenay oonah mesah mus taimpranoh/tarday

My name is...
Me llamo...
may yamoh

My telephone number is...
Mi número de teléfono es...
mee noomeroh day telefonoh es

I have a reservation
Tengo una reserva
taingoh oonah reserbah

in the name of...
a nombre de...
ah nombray day

We haven't booked
No tenemos reserva
noh tainemos reserbah

May we sit here?
¿Podemos sentarnos aquí?
podemos saintarnos ahkee

We'd like a table near the window
Quisiéramos una mesa cerca de la ventana
keesyeramos oonah mesah therkah day lah bentanah

We'd like to eat outside
Quisiéramos comer fuera
keesyeramos komair fwerah

ORDERING A MEAL

May we see the menu?	¿Nos trae la carta?
	nos tra-ay lah kartah
...the wine list?	...la carta de vinos?
	lah kartah day beenos
Do you have...	¿Tienen...
	tyenain
...a set menu?	...un menú del día?
	oon menoo dail deeyah
...a fixed-price menu?	...un menú a precio fijo?
	oon menoo ah prethyo feehoh
...a children's menu?	...un menú para niños?
	oon menoo parah neenyos
...an à la carte menu	...un menú a la carta?
	oon menoo ah lah kartah
What are today's specials?	¿Cuál es el plato del día?
	kwal es el plahto del deeyah
What are the local specialties?	¿Cuáles son los platos típicos?
	kwales son los plahtos teepeekos
What do you recommend?	¿Qué recomienda?
	kay raikomyendah

YOU MAY HEAR...

¿Tiene una reserva?
tyenay oonah reserbah
Do you have a reservation?

¿A nombre de quién?
ah nombray day kyen
In what name?

Tomen asiento
tomain ahsyentoh
Please be seated

¿Están listos para pedir?
estan leestos parah paideer
Are you ready to order?

What is this?	¿Qué es esto? *kay es estoh*
Are there any vegetarian dishes?	¿Hay platos vegetarianos? *ah-ee plahtos behetaryanos*
I can't eat...	No puedo comer... *noh pwedoh komair*
...dairy foods	...productos lácteos *prodooktos laktai-os*
...nuts	...frutos secos *frootos sekos*
...wheat	...trigo *treegoh*
To drink, I'll have...	Para beber, tomaré... *parah bebair tomaray*
May we have...	¿Nos trae... *nos tra-ay*
...some water?	...agua? *awu*
...some bread?	...pan? *pan*
...the dessert menu?	...la carta de postres? *lah kartah day postrais*

READING THE MENU...

| entrantes
entrantais
appetizers | segundos platos
saigoondos plahtos
main courses | quesos
kaisos
cheeses |
| primeros platos
preemeros plahtos
first courses | verduras
berdooras
vegetables | postres
postrais
desserts |

COMPLAINING

I didn't order this	Esto no es lo que he pedido *estoh noh es loh kay eh paideedoh*
When is our food coming?	¿Cuándo nos servirán la comida? *kwandoh nos serbeeran lah komeedah*
We can't wait any longer	No podemos esperar más *noh podemos esperar mas*

PAYING

The check, please	La cuenta, por favor *lah kwentah por fabor*
Can we pay separately?	¿Podemos pagar por separado? *podemos pagar por saiparadoh*
May I have...	¿Me da... *may dah*
...a receipt?	...un comprobante? *oon komprobantay*
...an itemized bill?	...una cuenta desglosada? *oonah kwentah daisglosadah*
Is service included?	¿Está incluido el servicio? *Estah eenklooydoh el serbeethyo*

YOU MAY HEAR...

No aceptamos tarjetas de crédito
noh ahtheptamos tarhetas day kredeetoh
We don't take credit cards

Por favor, introduzca su pin
por fabor eentrodoothkah soo peen
Please enter your PIN

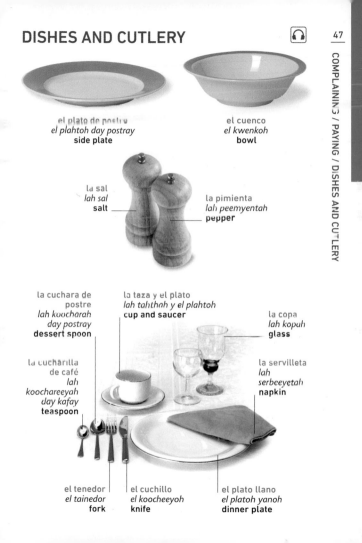

el plato de postre
el plahtoh day postray
side plate

el cuenco
el kwenkoh
bowl

la sal
lah sal
salt

la pimienta
lah peemyentah
pepper

la cuchara de postre
lah koocharah day postray
dessert spoon

la taza y el plato
lah tahthah y el plahtoh
cup and saucer

la copa
lah kopuh
glass

la cucharilla de café
lah koochareeyah day kafay
teaspoon

la servilleta
lah serbeeyetah
napkin

el tenedor
el tainedor
fork

el cuchillo
el koocheeyoh
knife

el plato llano
el plahtoh yanoh
dinner plate

AT THE CAFÉ OR BAR

The menu, please	La carta, por favor *lah kartah por fabor*
Do you have...?	¿Tienen...? *tyenain*
What fruit juices/herbal teas do you have?	¿Qué zumos de frutas/infusiones tienen? *kay thoomos day frootas/eenfoosyonais tyenain*
I'd like...	Quisiera... *keesyerah*
I'll have...	Tomaré... *tomaray*

un café con leche
oon kafay kon lechay
coffee with milk

un café solo
oon kafay soloh
black coffee

un cortado
oon kortadoh
**black coffee with
dash of milk**

un chocolate a la taza
*oon chokolatay ah
lah tathah*
hot chocolate

YOU MAY HEAR...

¿Qué van a tomar?
kay ban ah tomar
What would you like?

¿Algo más?
algoh mas
Anything else?

De nada
day nadah
You're welcome

un té con leche
oon tuy kon lechay
tea with milk

un té con limón
oon tay kon leemon
tea with lemon

un poleo
oon poleoh
mint tea

un té verde
oon tay berday
green tea

una manzanilla
oonah manthaneeyah
chamomile tea

una horchata
oonah orchatuh
tiger nut milk

A bottle of...	Una botella de... *oonah botaiyah day*
A glass of...	Un vaso de/una copa de... *oon basoh day/oonah kopah day*
A cup of...	Una taza de... *oonuh tathah day*
With lemon/milk	Con limón/leche *kon leemon/lechay*
Another...please	Otro...por favor *otroh...por fabor*
The same again, please	Lo mismo, por favor *loh meesmoh por fabor*

CAFÉ AND BAR DRINKS

un zumo de piña
*oon thoomoh
day peenyah*
pineapple juice

un zumo de manzana
*oon thoomoh
day manthanah*
apple juice

un zumo de naranja
*oon thoomoh
day naranhah*
fresh orange juice

una limonada
oonah leemonadah
lemonade

un mosto
oon mostoh
grape juice

un zumo de tomate
*oon thoomoh
day tomatay*
tomato juice

un café helado
oon kafay ehladoh
iced coffee

una cola
oonah kolah
cola

un tinto con gaseosa
oon teentoh kon gaseosah
red wine and lemonade

una naranjada
oonah naranhadah
orangeade

una jarra de sangría
oonah harrah day sangrya
jug of sangria

una cerveza
oonah thairbaithah
beer

agua mineral
awa meeneral
mineral water

una copa de jerez
oonah kopah day hairaith
glass of sherry

el vino blanco
el beenoh blankoh
white wine

un vino tinto
oon beenoh teentoh
red wine

YOU MAY HEAR...

¿Con gas o sin gas?
kon gas oh seen gas
Still or sparkling?

¿Con hielo?
kon yeloh
With ice?

¿Una caña?
oonah kanyah
A half?

¿En botella o de barril?
en botaiyah oh day barreel
Bottled or draft?

BAR SNACKS

el bocadillo
el bokadeeyoh
sandwich

los frutos secos
los frootos saikos
nuts

las aceitunas
las ahthaytoonas
olives

la tortilla
lah torteeyah
omelet

el aliño
el ahleenyoh
dressing

la ensalada
lah ensaladah
salad

el chorizo
el choreethoh
chorizo

las tapas (albóndigas)
las tapas (albondeegas)
tapas (meatballs)

el helado
el ehladoh
ice cream

las pastas
las pastas
pastry

FAST FOOD

May I have...

¿Me da...
may dah

...to eat in/carry out

...para comer aqui/para llevar
parah komair ahkee/ parah yebar

...some ketchup/mustard

...ketchup/mostaza
ketchoop/mostathah

la hamburguesa
lah amboorguisah
hamburger

la hamburguesa
de pollo
*lah amboorgaisah
day poyoh*
chicken burger

el rollo
el rollo
wrap

el frankfurt
el frankfoort
hot dog

el pinchito
el peencheetoh
kebab

las patatas fritas
las patatas freetas
French fries

el pollo frito
el poyoh freetoh
fried chicken

la pizza
lah peetsah
pizza

BREAKFAST

May I have...	¿Me trae... *may tra-ay*
...some milk	...leche? *lechay*
...some sugar	...azúcar? *ahthookar*
...some artificial sweetener	...edulcorante artificial? *edoolkorantay arteefeethyal*
...some butter	...mantequilla? *mantaikeeyah*
... some jam?	...confitura? *konfeetoorah*

un café
oon kafay
coffee

un té
oon tay
tea

un chocolate a
la taza
*oon chokolatay
ah lah tathah*
hot chocolate

un zumo de
naranja
*oon thoomoh day
naranhah*
orange juice

un zumo de
manzana
*oon thoomoh day
manthanah*
apple juice

el pan
el pan
bread

un panecillo
oon panetheeyoh
bread roll

los churros
los choorros
churros

un cruasán
oon crwusun
croissant

una mermelada
oonah mermeladah
marmalade

la miel
la myail
honey

los huevos
revueltos
*los webos
rebweltos*
**scrambled
eggs**

un huevo duro
*oon weboh
dooroh*
boiled egg

un huevo
escalfado
*oon weboh
eskalfadoh*
poached egg

un yogurt
de frutas
*oon yogoort
day frootas*
fruit yogurt

la fruta fresca
*lah frootah
fraiskah*
fresh fruit

FIRST COURSES

la sopa
lah sopah
soup

el caldo
el kaldoh
broth

la sopa de pescado
lah sopah day peskadoh
fish soup

la sopa de ajo
lah sopah day aho
garlic soup

el gazpacho
el gathpachoh
gazpacho

las gambas a la plancha
las gambas ah lah planchah
grilled shrimp

los mejillones
los meheeyonais
mussels

el calamar frito
el kalamar freetoh
fried squid

el marisco frito
*el mareeskoh
freetoh*
fried seafood

la ensalada
de marisco
*lah ensaladah
day mareeskoh*
seafood salad

el pescado adobado
el peskadoh adobadoh
marinated fish

los huevos
rellenos de atún
*los webos rayenos
day atoon*
tuna stuffed eggs

el revuelto de gambas
*el raibweltoh day
gambas*
**scrambled egg
and prawns**

el suflé
el sooflay
soufflé

la tortilla
lah torteeyah
omelet

la tortilla de patatas
lah torteeyah day patatas
Spanish omelet

los tomates
rellenos
*los tomatais
rayenos*
stuffed tomato

las berenjenas
rellenas
*lus berenhenas
rayenas*
stuffed eggplants

el jamón serrano
el hamon sairanoh
cured ham

los entremeses
variados
*los entraimesais
baryados*
cold platter

MAIN COURSES 🎧

I would like...	Tráigame... *traygamay*	**roast**	asado/a *asadoh/ah*
...the chicken	...el pollo *el poyoh*	**baked**	al horno *al ornoh*
...the duck	...el pato *el patoh*	**broiled**	a la plancha *ah lah planchah*
...the lamb	...el cordero *el korderoh*	**on skewers**	en brocheta *en brochaitah*
...the pork	...el cerdo *el thairdoh*	**barbecued**	a la parrilla *ah lah parreeyah*
...the beef	...la ternera *lah ternerah*	**poached**	cocido a fuego lento *kotheedoh*
...the steak	...el filete *el feeletay*		*ah fwegoh lentoh*
...the veal	...la ternera lechal *lah ternerah laichal*	**boiled**	hervido/a *erbeedoh/ah*
...the liver	...el hígado *el eegadoh*	**fried**	frito/a *freetoh/ah*

YOU MAY SEE...

marisco
mareeskoh
seafood

pescado
peskadoh
fish

YOU MAY HEAR...

¿Cómo quiere el filete?
komoh kyeray el feeletay
How do you like your steak?

¿Poco hecho, bien hecho?
pokoh echoh byen echoh
Rare or medium?

¿Muy hecho?
mooy echoh
Well done?

pan-fried/ **sautéed**	frito/salteado *freeetoh/saltai-ah doh*	**stewed**	estofado/a *aistofadoh/ah*
stuffed	relleno/a *rayenoh/ah*	**with cheese**	con queso *kon kaisoh*

carne de ave
karnay day ahbay
poultry

carne
karnay
meat

SALADS AND SIDE DISHES

la ensalada
de lechuga
*lah ensaladah
day laichoogah*
**green
salad**

la ensalada
mixta
*lah ensaladah
meekstah*
mixed salad

las patatas
fritas
*las patatas
freetas*
fried potatoes

la menestra de
verduras
*lah menestrah
day berdooras*
**mixed
vegetables**

las patatas fritas
las patatas freetas
French fries

el arroz
el ahrroth
rice

la ensalada
de pan
*lah ensaladah
day pan*
bread salad

el arroz con
verduras
*el ahrroth kon
berdooras*
**rice with
vegetables**

los pimientos
rellenos
*los peemyentos
raiyenos*
**stuffed
peppers**

la berenjena
rellena
*lah berenhena
rayenah*
**stuffed
eggplant**

DESADERTS

I would like...
Tráigame...
traygamay

...with cream
...con nata
kon natah

...with ice cream
...con helado
kon ehladoh

...with chocolate sauce
...con chocolate deshecho
kon chocolatay daisechoh

el sorbete
el sorbetay
sherbet

el helado
el ehladoh
ice cream

el pastel
el pastail
cake

el flan
el flan
crème caramel

la tarta de
frutas
*lah tarta day
frootas*
fruit tart

las natillas
las nateeyas
**custard
pudding**

la mousse de
chocolate
*lah moos day
chokolatay*
**chocolate
mousse**

la crema
catalana
*lah kraimah
katalanah*
egg custard

PLACES TO STAY

Spain has a wide range of places to stay, depending
on your personal preference and budget. These range
from historic *paradores* and luxurious hotels to smaller,
family-run *pensiones* (guest houses) and basic *hostales*.
If you want a self-catering option, however, you can rent
a seaside villa or city apartment, or find a campsite
to park your camper van or put up your tent.

MAKING A RESERVATION

I'd like...	Quisiera...
	keesyerah
...to make a reservation	...hacer una reserva
	ahthair oonah reserbah
a double room	...una habitación doble
	oonah ahbeetathyon dohblay
...a room with two twin beds	...una habitación con dos camas
	oonah ahbeetathyon kon dos kamas
...a single room	...una habitación individual
	oonah ahbeetathyon eendeebeedwal
...a family room	...una habitación familiar
	oonah ahbeetathyon fameelyar
...with a bathtub/shower	con baño/ducha
	kon banyoh/doochah
...with a sea view	...con vistas al mar
	kon beestas al mar
...with a balcony	...con balcón
	kon balkon
...for two nights	...para dos noches
	parah dos nochais
...for a week	...para una semana
	parah oonah semanah
Is breakfast included?	¿El desayuno está incluido en el precio?
	el daisayoonoh estah eenclooydoh en el prethyo
How much is it...	¿Cuánto cuesta...
	kwanto kwestah
...per night?	...por noche?
	por nochay
...per week?	...por semana?
	por semanah

CHECKING IN

I have a reservation	Tengo una reserva. *taingoh oonah reserbah*
Do you have...	¿Hay... *ah-ee*
I'd like...	Quisiera... *keesyerah*
...the keys for room...	...la llave de la habitación... *lah yabay day lah ahbeetathyon*
...a wake-up call at...	...que me despierten por la mañana a las... *kay meh despyertain por lah manyanah ah las*
What time is...	¿A qué hora se sirve... *ah kay ohrah say seerbay*
...breakfast?	...el desayuno? *el daisayoonoh*

un botones
oon botonais
porter

servicio de
habitaciones
*serbeethyo day
ahbeetathyones*
room service

el minibar
el meeneebar
mini bar

ascensores
asthensorais
elevators

IN YOUR ROOM

Do you have... ¿Tiene...
tyenay

another... otro/a ...
ohtroh/ah

some more... más...
mas

I've lost my key He perdido la llave
eh pairdeedoh la yabay

las mantas
las mantas
blankets

las almohadas
las almoadas
pillows

un adaptador
oon ahdaptador
adapter

una bombilla
oonah bombeeyah
light bulb

YOU MAY HEAR...

El número de su habitación es...
el noomeroh day soo ahbeetathyon es
Your room number is...

Aquí tiene la llave
ahkee tyenay lah yabay
Here is your key

IN THE HOTEL

The room is...	En la habitación hace... *en lah ahbeetathyon ahthay*
...too hot	...demasiado calor *demasyadoh kalor*
...too cold	...demasiado frío *demasyadoh freeyo*
The room is too small	La habitación es demasiado pequeña *lah ahbeetathyon es demasyadoh pekenya*
The window won't open	La ventana no se abre *la bentanah noh say abray*
What is the wifi code?	¿Cuál es la contraseña de la wifi? *kwal es lah kontrahsainyah day lah weefee*
The TV doesn't work	El televisor no funciona *el telebeesor noh foonthyonah*

el termostato
el termostatoh
thermostat

el radiador
el radyador
radiator

el hervidor de agua
el erbeedor day awa
kettle

la habitación
individual
*la ahbeetathyon
eendeebeedwal*
single room

la habitación doble
*lah ahbeetathyon
dohblay*
double room

El número de
la habitación
*el noomeroh day la
ahbeetathyon*
room number

el televisor
el telebeesor
television

el mando a distancia
el mandoh ah deestanthya
remote control

la percha
lah perchah
coat hanger

la persiana de
lamas
*lah persyanah
day lamas*
Venetian blind

CHECKING OUT

When do I have to vacate the room?	¿Cuándo hay que dejar la habitación? *kwandoh ah-ee kay dehar lah ahheetathyon*
Is there a porter to carry my bags?	¿Hay un botones para llevarme las maletas? *ah-ee oon botonais parah yebarmuy las maletahs*
May I have the bill, please	¿Me da la cuenta, por favor? *meh dah lah kwentah por fabor*
Can I pay by credit card?	¿Puedo pagar con tarjeta de crédito? *pwedoh pagar kon tarhetah day kredeetoh*
I'd like a receipt	¿Podría darme un comprobante? *podrya darmay oon komprobantay*

IN THE BATHROOM

las toallas
las toah-yas
towels

el albornoz
el albornoth
bathrobe

el jabón
el habon
soap

el desodorante
el desodorantay
deodorant

el dentífrico
el denteefreekoh
toothpaste

el baño de
burbujas
*el banyo day
boorboohas*
bubblebath

el bidé
el beeday
bidet

el gel de ducha
el hel day doochah
shower gel

la bañera
lah banyerah
bathtub

la loción
corporal
*lah lothyon
korporal*
body lotion

el cepillo de dientes
el thepeeyoh day dyentes
toothbrush

el secador de pelo
el sekador day peloh
blow-dryer

la maquinilla eléctrica
lah makeeneeya elektreekah
electric razor

la espuma de afeitar
lah espoomah day ahfeytar
shaving foam

la maquinilla
de afeitar
lah makeeneeya day ahfeytar
razor

el enjuague bucal
el enhwagay bookal
mouthwash

el champú
el champoo
shampoo

el suavizante
el swabeethantay
conditioner

el cortaúñas
el kortaoonyas
nail clippers

las tijeras
para las uñas
las teeheras parah las oonyas
nail scissors

SELF-CATERING

May we have...	¿Me da... *meh dah*
...the key, please?	...la llave, por favor? *lah yabay por fabor*
...an extra bed?	...una cama supletoria? *oonah kamah sooplaitoreeah*
...a child's bed?	...una camita de niño? *oonah kameetah day neenyoh*
...more cutlery/ dishes	...más cubiertos/vajilla *mas koobyertos/baheeyah*
Where is...	¿Dónde está... *donday estah*
...the fusebox?	...la caja de los plomos? *lah kahah day los plomos*
...the water valve?	...la llave de paso? *lah yabay day pasoh*

la estufa eléctrica
lah estoofah elektreekah
space heater

el ventilador
el benteelador
fan

la cuna
la kunah
crib

la trona
lah tronah
high chair

...the nearest doctor?	...el médico más cercano? *el medeekoh mas therkanoh*
...the nearest store?	... la tienda más cercana? *la tyendah mas therkanah*
Do you do babysitting?	¿Ofrecen servicio de canguro? *ofrethain serbeethyo day kangooroh*
How does the heating work?	¿Cómo funciona la calefacción? *komoh foonthyonah lah kalefakthyon*
Is there...	¿Hay... *ah-ee*
...air-conditioning?	...aire acondicionado? *aheeray ahkondeethyonado*
...central heating?	...calefacción central? *kalefakthyon thentral*
When does the cleaner come?	¿Cuándo vienen a limpiar? *kwandoh byenen ah leempyar*
Where do I put the garbage?	¿Dónde pongo la basura? *donday pongoh lah basoorah*
Who do we contact if there are problems?	¿A quién llamamos si hay problemas? *ah kyen yamamos see ah-ee problaimas*
Do you allow pets?	¿Aceptan animales domésticos? *ahtheptan ahneemalais domesteekos*

el perro
el perroh
dog

IN THE VILLA

Is there an inventory?
¿Hay un inventario?
ah-ee oon eenbentaryoh

Where is this item?
¿Dónde está este objeto?
donday estah estay obhetoh

I need...
Necesito...
netheseetoh

...an adapter
...un adaptador
oon ahdaptador

...an extension cord
...un alargador
oon ahlargador

...a flashlight
...una linterna
oonah leenternah

...matches
...cerillas
thereeyas

el microondas
el meekroondas
microwave

la plancha
lah planchah
iron

la tabla de planchar
lah tablah
day planchar
ironing board

la fregona y el cubo
lah fregonah ee el kooboh
mop and bucket

el recogedor
y el cepillo
el raikohedor
ee el thepeeyoh
dustpan and brush

el detergente
el daiterhentay
detergent

The shower doesn't work
La ducha no funciona
lah doochah noh foonthyona

The toilet is leaking
El váter tiene un escape
el bater tyenay oon escahpay

Can you fix it today?
¿Puede arreglarlo hoy?
pweday arreglarloh oi

There's no...
No hay...
noh ah-ee

...electricity
...electricidad
elektreetheedad

...water
...agua
awa

la lavadora
lah lubadorah
washing machine

el frigorífico
el freegoreefeekoh
refrigerator

el extintor
el eksteentor
fire extinguisher

la cerradura
y la llave
lah therradoorah
ee lah yabay
lock and key

la alarma de
incendios
lah alarmah day
eenthendyos
smoke alarm

el cubo de
la basura
el kooboh day
lah basoorah
trash can

KITCHEN EQUIPMENT

la tabla de cortar
lah tablah day kortar
cutting board

la bandeja de horno
lah bandeha day ohrnoh
cookie sheet

el batidor
el bateedor
whisk

el cuchillo de cocina
el koocheeyoh day kotheenah
kitchen knife

el pelador
el pailador
peeler

el abrelatas
el ahbrelatas
can opener

el abrebotellas
el ahbrebotaiyas
bottle opener

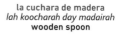

el sacacorchos
el sakakorchos
corkscrew

el rallador
el rayador
grater

la cuchara de madera
lah koocharah day madairah
wooden spoon

la sartén
lah sartain
frying pan

el colador
el kolador
colander

la espátula
lah espatoolah
spatula

la cacerola
lah katherolah
saucepan

la plancha
lah planchah
griddle pan

la olla
lah ohyah
casserole dish

el bol
el bohl
mixing bowl

el delantal
el dailantal
apron

las manoplas para el horno
las manoplas parah el ohrnoh
oven mitts

la licuadora
lah leekwadorah
blender

CAMPING

🎧

Where is the nearest...	**¿Dónde está el...** *donday estah el*
...campsite?	**...camping más cercano?** *kampeeng mas therkanoh*
...camper van site?	**...camping para caravanas más cercano?** *kampeeng parah karabanas mas therkanoh*
Can we camp here?	**¿Podemos acampar aquí?** *podemos ahkampar ahkee*
Do you have any vacancies?	**¿Tiene parcelas libres?** *tyenay parthelas leebrais*
What is the charge...	**¿Cuánto cuesta...** *kwanto kwestah*
...per night?	**...por noche?** *por nochay*
...per week?	**...por semana?** *por semanah*
Does the price include...	**¿El precio incluye...** *el prethyo eenklooyay*
...electricity?	**...la electricidad?** *lah elektreetheedad*
...hot water?	**...el agua caliente?** *el awa kalyentay*
We want to stay for...	**Queremos quedarnos...** *keremos kedarnos*

la tienda
lah tyendah
tent

la cuerda tensora
lah kwerdah tensorah
guy rope

la piqueta
lah peeketah
tent peg

Can I rent...	¿Se puede alquilar... *say pweday alkeelar*
...a tent?	...una tienda? *oonah tyendah*
...a barbecue?	...una barbacoa? *oonah barbakoah*
Where are...	¿Dónde están... *donday estan*
...the restrooms?	...los aseos? *los ahsaios*
...the garbage cans?	...los cubos de la basura? *los koobos day lah basoorah*
Are there...	¿Hay... *ah-ee*
...showers?	... duchas? *dochas*
...laundry facilities?	...servicios de lavandería? *serbeethyos day labanderya*
Is there...	¿Hay... *ah-ee*
...a swimming pool?	...piscina? *peestheenah*
...a store?	...una tienda? *oonah tyendah*

YOU MAY HEAR...

Está prohibido hacer fuego.
estah proybeedoh ahthair fwegoh
Don't light a fire

El agua no es potable.
el awa noh es potablay
Don't drink the water

AT THE CAMPSITE

cesta de picnic
*thaistah day
peekneek*
picnic basket

el termo
el tairmoh
vacuum flask

el hervidor de
agua para camping
*el erbeedor day
awa parah kampeeng*
camping kettle

el
impermeable
el eempermayablay
slickers

el agua embotellada
el awa emboteyadah
bottled water

el hornillo
el ohrneeyoh
camping stove

la nevera
lah naibairah
cooler

la barbacoa
lah barbakoah
barbecue

el colchón
hinchable
*el kolchon
eenchablay*
air mattress

el saco
de dormir
*el sakoh
day dormeer*
sleeping bag

la linterna
lah leenternah
flashlight

la mochila
lah mocheelah
backpack

el cubo
el kooboh
bucket

el mazo
el mahthoh
mallet

el repelente
de insectos
*el repelentay
day eensektos*
insect repellent

la crema con
filtro solar
*lah kremah kon
feeltroh sohlar*
sunscreen

la tirita
lah teereetah
**adhesive
bandage**

el ovillo
de cordel
*el ohbeeyoh
day kordel*
ball of string

las botas para
caminar
*las botas parah
kameenar*
hiking boots

la brújula
lah broohoolah
compass

SHOPPING

As well as department stores, supermarkets, and specialist shops, Spain has many picturesque open-air markets, held in town squares and on main streets, where you can buy fruit, vegetables, and regional specialities. Most shops close between 2 p.m. and 5 p.m. for the siesta but they do stay open quite late in the evenings. However, many small stores and food shops shut on Saturday afternoons, and few stores open on Sundays.

IN THE STORE

I'm looking for...

Estoy buscando...
estoy booskandoh

Do you have...?

¿Tiene...?
tyenay

I'm just looking

Sólo estoy mirando
soloh estoy meerandoh

I'm being served

Ya me atienden
yah may ahtyendain

Do you have any more of these?

¿Tiene otros más como éste?
tyenay ohtros mas komoh estay

How much is this?

¿Cuánto vale esto?
kwantoh balay estoh

Have you anything
cheaper?

¿Tiene otro más barato?
tyenay ohtroh mas baratoh

I'll take this one

Me llevo éste
may yeboh estay

Where can I pay?

¿Dónde hay que pagar?
donday ah-ee kay pagar

I'll pay...

Pagaré...
Pagaray

...in cash

...en efectivo
en efekteeboh

...by credit card

...con tarjeta de crédito
kon tarheta day kredeetoh

May I have a receipt?

¿Me da un comprobante?
may dah oon komprobantay

I'd like to exchange this

Quisiera descambiar esto
keesyerah deskambyar estoh

IN THE BANK

I'd like...	Quisiera... *keesyerah*
...to make a withdrawal	...sacar dinero *sakar deeneroh*
...to deposit some money	...ingresar dinero *eengresar deeneroh*
...to change some money	...cambiar dinero *kambyar deeneroh*
...into euros	...en euros *en eh-ooros*
...into dollars/sterling	...a dolares/en libras *ah dollarays/en leebras*
Here is my passport	Tenga mi pasaporte *tengah mee pasaporteh*
My name is...	Me llamo... *may yamoh*
My account number is...	El número de mi cuenta es... *el noomeroh day mee kwentah es*
My bank details are...	Mis datos bancarios son... *mees dahtos bankaryos son*

el pasaporte
el pasaportay
passport

el dinero
eel denaroh
money

el tipo de cambio
el teepoh day kambyoh
exchange rate

Do I have to...	¿Tengo que...
	taingoh kay
...key in my PIN?	...introducir mi pin?
	eentrodootheer mee peen
...sign here?	...firmar aquí?
	feermar ahkee
Is there a cash machine?	¿Hay un cajero automático?
	ah ee oon kaheroh ah-ootomateekoh
Can I withdraw money on my credit card?	¿Puedo sacar dinero a cuenta de mi tarjeta de crédito?
	pwedoh sakar deeneroh ah kwentah day mee tarhetah day kredeetoh
Can I cash a check?	¿Puedo cobrar un cheque?
	pwedoh kobrar oon chekay
When does the bank open/close?	¿Cuándo abre/cierra el banco?
	kwandoh ahbray/thyerrah el bankoh

el cajero
automático
*el kaheroh
ah-ootomateekoh*
cash machine

la tarjeta
de crédito
*lah tarhetah day
kredeetoh*
credit card

el talonario
de cheques
*el talonaryo
day chekais*
checkbook

STORES

la verdulería
lah berdoolerya
produce stand

la pescadería
lah peskaderya
fish seller

el colmado
el kolmadoh
grocery

la charcutería
lah charkooterya
delicatessen

la panadería
lah panaderya
baker

la librería
lah leebrerya
bookstore

el supermercado
el soopermerkadoh
supermarket

la carnicería
lah karneetherya
butcher

el estanco
el estankoh
tobacconist

la tienda de muebles
lah tyendah day mweblais
furniture store

la zapatería
lah thapaterya
shoe store

la boutique
lah bootik
boutique

la joyería
lah hoyairya
jewelry store

la sastrería
lah sastrerya
tailor

la ferretería
lah ferreterya
hardware store

AT THE MARKET

I would like...	Quisiera... *keesyerah*
How much is this?	¿Cuánto es? *kwantoh es*
What's the price per kilo?	¿A cuánto va el kilo? *ah kwantoh bah el keeloh*
It's too expensive	Es muy caro *es mooy karoh*
Do you have anything cheaper?	¿Tiene algo más barato? *tyenay algoh mas baratoh*
That's fine, I'll take it	Está bien, me lo llevo *estah byen may loh yeboh*
I'll take two kilos	Póngame dos kilos *pongamay dos keelos*
A kilo of...	Un kilo de... *oon keeloh day*
Half a kilo of...	Medio kilo de... *medyo keeloh day*
A little more, please	Un poco más, por favor *oon pokoh mas por fabor*
That's very good. I'll take some	Está muy bueno. Póngame un poco *estah mooy bwenoh pongameh oon pokoh*
That will be all, thank you	Nada más, gracias *nadah mas grathyas*

YOU MAY HEAR...

¿Qué desea? *kay daiseah* May I help you?	¿Cuánto le pongo? *kwantoh lay pongoh* How much would you like?

IN THE SUPERMARKET

Where is/are...	¿Dónde está/están... *donday estah/estan*
...the beverage aisle?	...el pasillo de las bebidas? *el paseeyoh day las beberdas*
...the checkout?	...las cajas? *las kahas*
I'm looking for...	Estoy buscando... *estoy booskandoh*
Do you have any more?	¿Tiene más? *tyenay mas*

el carrito
eel karrelloh
grocery cart

la cesta
lah thestah
basket

Is this reduced?	¿Está rebajado? *estah rebahadoh*
What is the sell-by date?	¿Qué fecha de caducidad tiene? *kay fechah day kadootheedad tyenay*
Where do I pay?	¿Dónde hay que pagar? *donday ahee kay pagar*
Shall I key in my PIN?	¿Introduzco el pin? *eentrodoothkoh el peen*
May I have a bag?	¿Me da una bolsa? *may day oonah bolsah*
Can you help me pack	¿Puede ayudarme a guardar en las bolsas? *pweday ahyoodarmay ah gwardar en las bolsas*

FRUIT

una naranja
oonah naranhah
orange

un limón
oon leemon
lemon

un melocotón
oon melokoton
peach

una nectarina
oonah nektareenah
nectarine

una lima
oonah leemah
lime

una cereza
oonah thairethah
cherries

un albaricoque
oon albareekokay
apricot

una ciruela
oonah theerwelah
plum

un pomelo
oon pomeloh
grapefruit

un arándano
oon ahrandanoh
blueberry

una fresa
oonah fresah
strawberry

una frambuesa
oonah frambwesah
raspberry

un melón
oon mailon
melon

las uvas
las oobas
grapes

un plátano
oon platanoh
banana

una granada
oonah granadah
pomegranate

una manzana
oonah manthanah
apple

una pera
oonah pairah
pear

una piña
oonah peenyah
pineapple

un mango
oon mangoh
mango

VEGETABLES

una patata
oonah patatah
potato

una zanahoria
oonah thanaohrya
carrot

un pimiento
oon peemyentoh
pepper

una guindilla
oonah gheendeeyah
chili pepper

una berenjena
oonah berenhainah
eggplant

un tomate
oon tohmatay
tomato

una cebolla
oonah thaiboyah
onion

un ajo
oon ahoh
garlic

una cebolleta
oonah theboyetah
scallion

un puerro
oon pwerroh
leek

un champiñón
oon champeenyon
mushroom

un calabacín
oon kalubatheen
zucchini

el guisante
el gheesantay
garden peas

una judía verde
oonah hoodeeah berday
green beans

un pepino
oon pepeenoh
cucumber

un apio
oon ahpeeoh
celery

una espinaca
oonah espeenakah
spinach

un brécol
oon brekol
broccoli

una lechuga
oonah lechoogah
lettuce

una col
oonah kol
cabbage

MEAT AND POULTRY

May I have...

...a slice of...?

...a piece of...?

¿Me pone...
may pohnay

...una loncha de...?
oonah lonchah day

...un trozo de...?
oon trothoh day

el jamón
el hamon
ham

la carne
picada
*lah karnay
peekadah*
ground beef

el filete
el feeletay
steak

las salchichas
las salcheechas
sausages

el cordero
el korderoh
lamb

el chorizo
el choreethoh
chorizo

el pollo
eel polloh
chicken

el pato
el patoh
duck

FISH AND SHELLFISH

el atún
el ahtoon
tuna

el calamar
el kalamar
squid

el bacalao
el bakalaoh
cod

la lubina
lah loobeenah
sea bass

el pargo
el pargoh
sea bream

la sardina
lah sardeenah
sardine

el cangrejo
el kangrehoh
crab

la langosta
lah langostuh
lobster

el pulpo
el poolpoh
octopus

la gamba
lah gambah
shrimp

BREAD AND CAKES

el pan blanco
el pan blankoh
white bread

la tortilla
lah torteeyah
tortilla

el cruasán
el crwasan
croissant

el panecillo
el panetheeyoh
roll

las galletas
las gayetas
cookies

la madalena
lah madalenah
sponge cake

el trozo de pastel
el trothoh day pastail
slice of cake

la ensaimada
lah ensaymadah
spiral bun

**la tartaleta
de frutas**
*lah tartaletah
day frootas*
fruit tart

**el pastel
de chocolate**
*el pastail day
chocolatay*
chocolate cake

DAIRY PRODUCE

la leche entera
lah lechay enterah
whole milk

la leche
semidesnatada
*lah lechay
semeedesnataduh*
reduced-fat milk

el yogurt
el yogoort
yogurt

la mantequilla
lah mantaikeeyah
butter

la nata
lah natah
cream

el queso rallado
el kaisoh rayadoh
grated cheese

el cabrales
el kabralais
Cabrales

el queso seco
el kaisoh saikoh
hard cheese

el queso de cabra
el kaisoh day kabrah
goat's cheese

el manchego
el manchaigoh
Manchego

NEWSPAPERS AND MAGAZINES

Do you have... ¿Tiene...
tyenay

...a book of stamps? ...sellos?
seyos

...airmail stamps? ...sellos de correo por avión?
seyos day korreoh por ahbyon

...a pack of envelopes? ...un paquete de sobres?
oon paketay day sobrais

...some adhesive tape? ...cinta adhesiva?
theentah adeseebah

una postal
oonah postal
postcard

un lápiz
oon lapeeth
pencil

unos sellos
oonos sayos
stamps

un bolígrafo
oon boleegrafoh
pen

YOU MAY HEAR...

¿Tiene un documento de identidad?
tyenay oon dokoomentoh day eedenteedad
Do you have ID?

¿Cuántos años tiene?
kwantos ahnyos tyenay
How old are you?

I'd like...

Quisiera...
keesyerah

...a pack of cigarettes

...un paquete de tabaco
oon paketay day tabukoh

...a box of matches

...una caja de cerillas
oonah kahah day thereeyas

un tebeo
oon taibeoh
comic book

un mechero
oon mecheroh
lighter

unos lápices de colores
*oonos lapeethais
day kolorais*
colored pencils

un chicle
oon cheeclay
chewing gum

unos caramelos
oonos karamelos
candy

tabaco de liar
tabakoh day lee-ar
tobacco

unas revistas
oonas raibeestas
magazine

un periódico
oon peryodeekoh
newspaper

BUYING CLOTHES AND SHOES

I am looking for...
Estoy buscando...
estoy booskandoh

I am size...
Gasto la talla...
gastoh lah tayah

Do you have this...
¿Tiene éste...
tyenay estay

...in my size?
...en mi talla?
en mee tayah

...in small
...en la talla pequeña?
en lah tayah pekenya

...in medium?
...en la talla mediana?
en lah tayah medyanah

...in large?
...en la talla grande?
en lah tayah granday

...in other colors?
...en otros colores?
en ohtros kolorais

May I try this on?
¿Puedo probármelo?
pwedoh probarmailoh

It's...
Es...
es

...too big
...muy grande
mooy granday

...too small
...muy pequeño
mooy pekenyoh

I need...
Necesito...
netheseetoh

...a larger size
...una talla más
oonah tayah mas

...a smaller size
... una talla menos
oonah tayah menos

I'll take this one, please
Me llevo éste
may yeboh estay

I take shoe size...	Calzo el número... *kalthoh el noomeroh*
May I try...	¿Puedo probarme... *pwedoh probarmay*
...this pair?	...este par? *estay par*
...those in the window?	...los del escaparate? *los dail aiskaparatay*
These are...	Me quedan... *may kedan*
...too tight	...muy estrechos *mooy estrechos*
...too big	...muy grandes *mooy grandais*
...too small	... muy pequeños *mooy pekenyos*
These are uncomfortable	Son incómodos *son eenkomodos*
Is there a bigger size?	¿Tienen un número más? *tyenain oon noomeroh mus*

CLOTHES AND SHOE SIZES GUIDE

Women's clothes sizes	US	4	6	8	10	12	14	16	18
	Europe	34	36	38	40	42	44	46	48
Men's clothes sizes	US	36	38	40	42	44	46	48	50
	Europe	46	48	50	52	54	56	58	60
Shoe sizes	US	5	4	7	8	9	10	11	12	13
	Europe	36	67	38	39	40	42	43	45	46

CLOTHES AND SHOES

el vestido
el baisteedoh
dress

el vestido de noche
el baisteedoh day nochay
evening dress

la chaqueta
lah chakaitah
jacket

el jersey
el hairsey
sweater

los tejanos
los tehanos
jeans

la falda
lah faldah
skirt

la bambas
lah bambas
sneakers

la bota
lah bohtah
boots

el bolso
el bolsoh
handbag

el cinturón
el theentooron
belt

el traje
el trahay
suit

el abrigo
el abreegoh
coat

la camisa
lah kameesah
shirt

la camiseta
lah kameesetah
T-shirt

los pantalones
cortos
*los pantalonais
kortos*
shorts

el zapato
de tacón
*el thapatoh
day takon*
**high-heeled
shoes**

el zapato
de cordones
*el thapatoh
day kordonais*
tie shoes

la sandalia
lah sandalyah
sandals

la chancla
lah chanclah
flip-flops

los
calcetines
*los
kaltheteenais*
socks

AT THE GIFT SHOP

I'd like to buy a gift for...	Quisiera comprar un regalo para... *keesyerah komprar oon regaloh parah*
...my mother/father	...mi madre/padre *mee madray/padray*
...my daughter/son	...mi hija/hijo *mee eehah/eehoh*
...a child	...un niño *oon neenyoh*
...a friend	...un amigo *oon ahmeegoh*
Can you recommend something?	¿Qué me recomienda? *kay may raikomyendah*
Do you have a box for it?	¿Viene con caja? *byenay kon kahah*
Can you gift-wrap it?	¿Podría envolverlo para regalo? *Podryah enbolberloh parah regaloh*
Do you sell wrapping paper?	¿Venden papel de envolver? *benden papail day enbolbair*

una pulsera
oonah poolserah
bracelet

un collar
oon koyar
necklace

un reloj
oon reloh
watch

unos gemelos
oonos hemelos
cufflinks

una cartera
oonah karterah
wallet

una muñeca
oonah moonyekah
doll

un peluche
oon peloochay
stuffed animal

unos bombones
oonos bombonos
chocolates

Have you anything cheaper?	¿Tiene algo más barato? *tyenay algoh mas baratoh*
Is there a reduction for cash?	¿Hacen descuento por pago en efectivo? *ahthain deskwentoh por pagoh en efekteeboh*
Is there a guarantee?	¿Tiene garantía? *tyenay garantyah*
May I exchange this?	¿Puedo descambiarlo? *pwedoh deskambyarloh*

YOU MAY HEAR...

¿Es para regalo?
es parah regaloh
Is it for a present?

¿Se lo envuelvo para regalo?
say loh enbwelboh parah regaloh
Shall I gift-wrap it?

PHOTOGRAPHY

I'd like this film developed	Quisiera revelar este carrete *keesyera rebelar estay karretay*
When will it be ready?	¿Cuándo estará listo? *kwandoh estarah leestoh*
Do you have an express service?	¿Tiene servicio de revelado rápido? *tyenay serbeethyoh day rebeladoh rapeedoh*
I'd like the one-hour service	Quisiera el servicio de revelado en una hora *keesyera el serbeethyo day rebeladoh en oona ohrah*

una cámara
digital
*oonah kamarah
deeheetal*
digital camera

una tarjeta de
memoria
*oonah tarhetah
day memohryah*
memory card

un marco
para fotos
*oon markoh
parah fohtos*
photo frame

un álbum de fotos
*oon alboom day
fohtos*
photo album

I'd like a battery

Quisiera una pila
keesyera oonah peelah

Can you print from this memory stick?

¿Puede imprimir de esta llave USB?
pweday eempreemeer day estah yabay oo essay bay

un objetivo
oon obheteeboh
lens

una cámara
oonah kamarah
camera

una funda de la cámara
oonah foondah day lah kamarah
camera bag

un flash
oon flash
flash gun

YOU MAY HEAR...

¿Qué tamaño de fotos quiere?
kay tamanyoh day fohtos kyeray
What size prints do you want?

¿Mate o brillante?
matay o breeyantay
Matte or gloss?

¿Para cuándo las quiere?
parah kwando las kyeray
When do you want them?

AT THE POST OFFICE

I'd like...

Quisiera...
keesyerah

...three stamps, please

...tres sellos, por favor
trais saiyos, por fabor

...to register this letter

...certificar esta carta
therteefeekar estah kartah

...to send this airmail

...enviar esto por avión
enbeear estoh por ahbyon

unos sellos
oonos sayos
stamps

un sobre
oon sobray
envelope

por avión
por ahbyon
airmail

una postal
oonah postal
postcard

YOU MAY HEAR...

¿Qué contiene?
kay kontyenay
What are the contents?

¿Qué valor tiene?
kay balor tyenay
What is their value?

Rellene este impreso
reyenay estay eempresoh
Fill out this form

How much is...?	¿Cuánto cuesta... *kwantoh kwestah*
...a letter to...	...enviar una carta a... *enbeear oonah kartah ah*
...a postcard to...	...enviar una postal a... *enbeear oonah postal ah*
...the United States	...Estados Unidos *estados ooneedos*
...Great Britain	...Gran Bretaña *gran braitanyah*
...Canada	...Canadá *kanaduh*
...Australia	...Australia *ah-oostralyah*
May I have a receipt?	¿Me da un comprobante? *may dah oon komprohantay*
Where can I mail this?	¿Dónde se echa esto al correo? *donday say echah estoh al korraio*

un paquete
oon paketay
package

el mensajero
el mensaheroh
courier

un buzón
oon boothon
mailbox

el cartero
el karteroh
letter carrier

TELEPHONES

Where is the nearest phone shop?	¿Dónde está la tienda de telefonía más cercana? *donday estah lah tyendah day tailaifoneeah mas thairkanah*
Who's speaking?	¿Quién llama? *kyen yamah*
Hello, this is...	Hola, soy... *ohlah soy*
I'd like to speak to...	Quisiera hablar con... *keesyerah ahblar kon*
May I leave a message?	¿Puedo dejarle un mensaje? *pwedoh deharlay oon mensahay*

el teléfono inalámbrico
el telefonoh eenalambreekoh
cordless phone

el teléfono
inteligente
*el telefonoh
eentaileehaintay*
smartphone

el móvil
el mobeel
cell phone

el contestador automático
el kontestador ah-ootomateekoh
answering machine

el teléfono
de monedas
*el telefonoh
day monedas*
**coin-operated
phone**

INTERNET

Is there an internet café near here?	¿Hay un cibercafé por aquí cerca? *ah-ee oon theebercafay por ahkee therkah*
How much do you charge?	¿Cuánto cobran? *kwuntoh kobrun*
Do you have wireless internet?	¿Tienen conexión inalámbrica a Internet? *tyenain koneksyon eenalambreekah ah internet*
Can I check my emails?	¿Puedo comprobar mis emails? *pwedoh komporbar mees eemaeels*
I need to send an email	Tengo que enviar un email *taingoh kay enbeear oon eemaeel*
What's your email address?	¿Cuál es su dirección de email? *kwal es soo deerekthyon day eemaeel*
My email address is...	Mi dirección de email es... *mee deerekthyon day eemaeel es*

el portátil
el portateel
laptop

el teclado
el tekladoh
keyboard

el sitio web
el seetyo web
website

el email
el eemaeel
email

SIGHTSEEING

Most towns have a tourist information office and the staff will advise you on local places to visit and excursions. Many museums and art galleries close on Mondays as well as public holidays, so check the opening times before visiting. You will usually have to pay an admission fee, but some offer discounts to seniors, minors, and students.

Where is the tourist information office?	¿Dónde está la oficina de turismo? *donday estah alah ofeetheenah day tooreesmoh*
Can you recommend...	¿Puede recomendarme... *pweday raikomendarmay*
...a guided tour?	...una visita guiada? *oonah beeseetah geeyadah*
...an excursion?	...una excursión? *oonah ekskoorsyon*
Is there a museum or art gallery?	¿Hay un museo o una galería de arte? *ah-ee oon moosayoh oh oonah galerceyah day artay*
Is it open to the public?	¿Está abierto al público? *estah ahbyertoh al poohleekoh*
Is there wheelchair access?	¿Dispone de acceso para sillas de ruedas? *deesponay day akthaisoh parah seeyus day rwedas*
Does it close...	¿Cierra... *thyerah*
...on Sundays?	...los domingos? *los dohmeengos*
...on public holidays?	...los festivos? *los festeebos*
How long does it take to get there?	¿Cuánto se tarda en llegar? *kwantoh say tardah en yegur*
Do you have...	¿Tiene... *tyenay*
...a street map?	...un plano? *oon plahnoh*
...a guide?	...una guía? *oonah gheeyah*
...any leaflets?	...folletos? *fohyetos*

VISITING PLACES

What time...
¿A qué hora...
ah kay ohrah

...do you open?
...abren?
ahbrain

...do you close?
...cierran?
thyerran

I'd like two entrance tickets
Quisiera dos entradas
keesyerah dos entradas

Two adults, please
Dos adultos, por favor
dos ahdooltos por fabor

A family ticket, please
Una entrada familiar
oonah entradah fameelyar

How much does it cost?
¿Cuánto cuesta?
kwantoh kwestah

Are there reductions for...
¿Hacen descuento a...
ahthain deskwentoh ah

...children?
...los niños?
los neenyos

...students?
los estudiantes?
los estoodyantais

el plano
el planoh
street map

el acceso para sillas de ruedas
el akthaisoh parah seeyas day rwedas
wheelchair access

la oficina de turismo
lah ofeetheenah day tooreesmoh
tourist office

Can I buy a guidebook?	¿Puedo comprar una guía?
	pwedoh komprar oonah gheeyah
Is there...	¿Hay...
	_ah-ee_
...an audio-guide?	...guías en audio?
	gheeyas en ah-oodyo
...a guided tour?	...una visita guiada?
	oonah beeseetah gheeyadah
...an elevator?	...un ascensor?
	oon asthensor
...a bus tour?	...una excursión en autocar?
	oonah ekskoorsyon en ah-ootocar
...wheelchair access?	...acceso para sillas de ruedas?
	akthaisoh parah seeyas day rwedas
...a gift shop?	...una tienda de regalos?
	oonah tyendah day regalos

el autobús turístico
el ah-outoboos tooreesteekoh
tour bus

YOU MAY HEAR...

¿Tiene carné de estudiante?
tyenay karnay day estoodyantay
Do you have a student ID?

FINDING YOUR WAY

Excuse me	**Disculpe** *deeskoolpay*
Can you help me?	**¿Puede ayudarme?** *pweday ahyoodarmay*
Is this the way to...?	**¿Por aquí se va...** *por ahkee say bah*
How do I get to...?	**¿Cómo se va...** *komoh say bah*
...the town center?	**...al centro?** *al thentroh*
...the station?	**...a la estación?** *ah lah estathyon*
...the museum?	**...al museo?** *al moosayoh*
...the art gallery?	**...a la galería de arte?** *ah lah galereeyah day artay*
How long does it take?	**¿Cuánto se tarda?** *kwantoh say tardah*
Is it far?	**¿Está lejos?** *estah lehos*
Is it within walking distance?	**¿Se puede ir andando?** *say pweday eer andandoh*
Can you show me on the map?	**¿Puede indicármelo en el plano?** *pweday eendeekarmeloh en el planoh*

YOU MAY HEAR...

No está lejos
noh estah lehos
It's not far away

Se tardan diez minutos
say tardan deeyaith meenootos
It takes ten minutes

YOU MAY HEAR...

Estamos aquí
estamos ahkee
We are here

Siga todo recto...
seegah todoh rektoh
Keep going straight...

...hasta el final de la calle
astah el feenal day lah kayay
...to the end of the street

...hasta el semáforo
astah el saimaforoh
...to the traffic lights

...hasta la plaza
astah lah plathah
...to the main square

Por aquí
por ahkee
This way

Por allí
por ahyee
That way

Doble a la derecha en...
doblay ah lah derechah en
Turn right at...

Doble a la izquierda en...
doblay ah lah eethkyerdah en
Turn left at...

Coja la primera...
kohah lah preemerah
Take the first...

...a la izquierda/derecha
ah lah eethkyerdah/derechah
...on the left/right

Queda delante de usted
kedah dailantay day oosted
It's in front of you

Queda detrás de usted
kedah detras day oosted
It's behind you

Queda enfrente de usted
kedah ainfrentay day oosted
It's opposite you

Está al lado de...
estah al ladoh day
It's next to...

Está señalizado
estah senyaleethadoh
It's signed

Está por allí
estah por ahyee
It's over there

PLACES TO VISIT

el ayuntamiento
el ah-yoontamyentoh
town hall

el puente
el pwentay
bridge

el museo
el moosayoh
museum

la galería de arte
*lah galereeyah
day artay*
art gallery

el monumento
el monoomentoh
monument

la iglesia
la eeglesya
church

el pueblo
el pwebloh
village

la catedral
lah kataydral
cathedral

el castillo
el kasteeyoh
castle

el faro
el faroh
lighthouse

el puerto
el pwertoh
harbor

los viñedos
los beenyedos
vineyard

el parque
el parkay
park

la costa
la kostah
coast

la cascada
lah kaskadah
waterfall

las montañas
las montanyas
mountains

OUTDOOR ACTIVITIES

Where can we go...	¿Dónde podemos ir... *donday podemos eer*
...horseback riding?	...a montar a caballo? *ah montar ah kabayoh*
...fishing?	...a pescar? *ah peskar*
...swimming?	...a nadar? *ah nadar*
...walking?	...a pasear? *ah pasaiar*
Can we...	¿Podemos... *podemos*
...rent equipment?	...alquilar el equipo? *alkeelar el ekeepoh*
...take lessons?	...tomar clases? *tomar klasais*
How much per hour?	¿Cuánto cuesta a la hora? *kwantoh kwestah ah lah ohrah*
I'm a beginner	Soy principiante *soy preentheepyantay*
I'm very experienced	Tengo bastante experiencia *taingoh bastantay eksperyenthya*
Where's the amusement park?	¿Dónde está el parque de atracciones? *donday estah el parkay day atrakthyonais*
Can the children go on all the rides?	¿Los niños pueden subirse en todas las atracciones? *los neenyos pweden soobeersay en todas las atrakthyonais*
Is there a playground?	¿Hay columpios? *ah-ee koloompyos*
Is it safe for children?	¿Es seguro para los niños? *es segooroh parah los neenyos*

el zoológico
el tho-ohloheekuh
zoo

los columpios
los koloompyos
playground

el picnic
el peeknéek
picnic

el parque de atracciones
el parkay day atrakthyonais
fairground

la pesca
la peskah
fishing

montar a caballo
montar ah kabayoh
horseback riding

el safari
el safaree
safari park

el parque temático
el parkay taimateekoh
amusement park

SPORTS AND LEISURE

Spain can offer the traveler a wide range of cultural events, musical entertainments, leisure activities, and sports. You can swim or enjoy a range of watersports on the coast, hike, cycle, or ride in the national parks, or even go skiing in the mountains. Spain has some of the best golf courses in the world, especially on the sunny Costa del Sol. Although you rarely need to be a club member to play a round, it can be very expensive on the most famous courses.

LEISURE TIME

I like...	Me gusta... *may goostah*
...art and painting	...el arte y la pintura *el artay ee lah peentooruh*
...movies and film	...las películas y el cine *las peleekoolas ee el theenay*
...the theater	...el teatro *el tay-ahtroh*
...opera	...la ópera *lah ohperah*
I prefer...	Prefiero... *prefeeroh*
...reading books	...leer libros *lay uh leebros*
...listening to music	...escuchar música *eskoochar mooseekah*
...watching sports	...ver deporte *bair deportay*
...going to concerts	...ir a conciertos *eer uh konthyertos*
...dancing	...bailar *bah-eylar*
...going to clubs	...ir de discotecas *eer duy dyskotekas*
...going out with friends	...salir con los amigos *saleer kon los ahmeegos*
I don't like...	No me gusta... *noh may goostah*
That doesn't interest me	Eso no me interesa *esoh noh may eenteresah*

AT THE BEACH

Can I rent...
¿Puedo alquilar...
pwedoh alkeelar

...a jet ski?
...una moto acuática?
oonah motoh akwateekah

...a beach umbrella?
...un parasol?
oon parasol

...a surfboard?
...una tabla de surf?
oonah tablah day soorf

...a wetsuit?
...un traje de neopreno?
oon trahay day nayoprenoh

la toalla de playa
lah toah-yah day playah
beach towel

la hamaca
lah ahmakah
deck chair

la pelota hinchable
lah pelotah eenchablay
beach ball

la tumbona
lah toombonah
lounge chair

YOU MAY HEAR...

Prohibido bañarse
proybeedoh banyarsay
No swimming

Playa cerrada
playah theradah
Beach closed

Fuertes corrientes
fwertais koryentais
Strong currents

How much does it cost?	¿Cuánto cuesta? *kwanto kwestah*
Can I go water-skiing?	¿Puedo hacer esquí acuático? *pwedoh ahthair eskee akwateekoh*
Is there a lifeguard?	¿Hay socorristas? *ah-ee sokoreestas*
Is it safe to...	¿Es seguro... *es segooroh*
...swim here?	...bañarse aquí? *banyarsay ahkee*
...surf here?	...hacer surf aquí? *uhthair soorf ahkee*

las gafas de sol
las gafas day sol
sunglasses

el sombrero
el sombreroh
sun hat

las aletas
las ahlaitas
fins

el bronceador
el brontheahdor
suntan lotion

el bikini
el beekeenee
bikini

las gafas y el
tubo de buceo
*las gafas ee el
tooboh day boothaio*
mask and snorkel

AT THE SWIMMING POOL

What time...
¿A qué hora...
ah kay ohrah

...does the pool open?
...abre la piscina?
abray lah peestheenah

...does the pool close?
...cierra la piscina?
thyerah lah peestheenah

Is it...
¿Hay...
ah-ee

...an indoor pool?
...piscina cubierta?
peestheenah koobyertah

...an outdoor pool?
...piscina descubierta?
peestheenah deskoobyertah

Is there a children's pool?
¿Hay piscina infantil?
ah-ee peestheenah eenfanteel

Where are the changing rooms?
¿Dónde están los vestuarios?
donday estan los bestwaryos

Is it safe to dive?
¿Es seguro tirarse desde el trampolín?
es segooroh teerarsay dezday el trampoleen

los manguitos
los mangheetos
water wings

los flotadores
los flohtadohres
floats

las gafas de natación
las gafas day natathyon
swimming goggles

el bañador
el banyador
swimsuit

AT THE GYM

la bicicleta elíptica
*lah beetheekletah
eleepteekah*
cross trainer

la bicicleta
estática
*lah beetheekletah
estateekah*
exercise bike

la máquina de remo
lah makeenah day raimoh
rowing machine

el stepper
el esteppair
step machine

Is there a gym?	¿Hay gimnasio? *ah-ee heemnasyo*
Is it free for guests?	¿Es gratis para los huéspedes? *es gratees parah los wespedais*
Do I have to wear sneakers?	¿Tengo que llevar bambas? *tuingoh kay yebar bumbus*
Do I need an introductory session?	¿Es necesaria una sesión de introducción? *es nethesaryah oonah sesyon day centrodookthyon*
Do you hold...	¿Dan... *dan*
...aerobics classes?	...clases de aeróbic? *klasais day aherobeek*
...Pilates classes?	...clases de Pilates? *klasais day peelatais*
...yoga classes?	...clases de yoga? *klasais day yohgah*

BOATING AND SAILING

Can I rent...	¿Puedo alquilar... *pwedoh alkeelar*
...a dinghy?	...un bote? *oon botay*
...a windsurf board?	...una tabla de windsurf? *oonah tablah day windsoorf*
...a canoe?	...una canoa? *oonah kanoah*
...a rowboat?	...una barca de remos *oonah barkah day raimos*
Do you offer sailing lessons?	¿Dan clases de navegación? *dan klasais day nabegathyon*
Do you have a mooring?	¿Tienen atracadero? *tyenain ahtrakadairoh*
How much is it for the night?	¿Cuánto cuesta por noche? *kwantoh kwestah por nochay*
Where can I buy gas?	¿Dónde se puede comprar el gas? *donday say pweday komprar el gas*
Where is the marina?	¿Dónde está el puerto deportivo? *donday estah el pwertoh deporteeboh*
Are there life jackets?	¿Hay chalecos salvavidas? *ah-ee chalekos salbabeedas*

el chaleco
salvavidas
*el chalaikoh
salbabeedas*
life jacket

la brújula
lah broohoolah
compass

I would like to rent...	Quisiera alquilar... *keesyerah alkeelar*
...some skis	...unos esquíes *oonos eskyes*
...some ski boots	...unas botas de esquí *oonas bohtas day eskee*
...some poles	...unos bastones *oonos bastonais*
...a snowboard	...una tabla de snowboard *oonah tablah day esnowbord*
...a helmet	...un casco *oon kaskoh*
When does...	¿Cuándo... *Kwandoh*
...the chair lift start?	...empieza el telesilla? *empyethah el teleseeyah*
...the cable car finish?	...acaba el teleférico? *akabah el telefereekoh*
How much is a lift pass?	¿Cuánto cuesta un pase para el telesilla? *kwantoh kwestah oon pasay parah el teleseeyah*
Can I take skiing lessons?	¿Puedo tomar clases de esquí? *pwedoh tomar klasais day eskee*

YOU MAY HEAR...

¿Es usted principiante?
es oosted preentheepyanteh
Are you a beginner?

Hay que abonar una paga y señal
ah-ee kay ahbonar oonah pagah ee sainyal
I need a deposit

BALL GAMES

I like playing...	Me gusta jugar... *may goostah hoogar*
...soccer	...al fútbol *al footbol*
...tennis	...al tenis *al tenees*
...golf	...al golf *al golf*
...badminton	...al bádminton *al badmeenton*
...squash	...al squash *al eskwash*
Where is the nearest...	¿Dónde está... *donday estah*
...tennis court?	...la pista de tenis más cercana? *lah peestah day tenees mas therkanah*
...golf course?	...el campo de golf más cercano? *el kampoh day golf mas therkanoh*
What shoes are allowed?	¿Qué calzado está permitido? *kay kalthadoh estah permeeteedoh*

el balón de
fútbol
*el balón day
footbol*
soccer ball

la canasta
lah kanastah
basket

el guante de
béisbol
*el wantay day
beysbol*
baseball glove

May I book a court...	¿Puedo reservar una pista... *pwedoh reserbar oonah peestah*
...for two hours?	...para dos horas? *parah dos ohras*
...at three o'clock?	...a las tres? *ah las trais*
May I rent...	¿Puedo alquilar... *pwedoh alkeelar*
...a tennis racket?	...una raqueta de tenis? *oonah rakaitah day tenees*
...some balls?	...pelotas? *pailotas*
...a set of clubs?	...un juego de palos? *oon hoo-egoh day pahlos*
...a golf buggy?	...un buggy? *oon buggy*

las pelotas de tenis
las pailotas day tenees
tennis balls

el palo de golf
el pahloh day golf
golf club

la pelota y el
tee de golf
*lah pelotah ee el
tee day golf*
golf ball and tee

las muñequeras
las moonyekeras
wristbands

la raqueta de tenis
lah rakaitah day tenees
tennis racket

GOING OUT

Where is...	¿Dónde está... *donday estah*
...the opera house?	...el teatro de la ópera? *el tay-ahtroh day lah ohperah*
...a jazz club?	...un club de jazz? *oon kloob day jazz*
Do I have to book in advance?	¿Tengo que reservar con antelación? *Taingoh kay reserbar kon antelathyon*
I'd like...tickets	Deme...entradas *daymay...entradas*
I'd like seats...	Quisiera los asientos... *keesyerah los asyentos*
...at the back	...en el fondo *en el fondoh*
...at the front	...delante *daylantay*
...in the middle	...en el centro *en el thentroh*
...in the balcony	...en el gallinero *en el gayeeneroh*
Can I buy a program?	¿Puedo comprar un programa? *Pwedoh komprar oon programah*

YOU MAY HEAR...

Apaguen los móviles
Apaghen los mobeelais
Turn off your cell phone

Regresen a sus asientos
Raygresain ah soos ahsyentos
Return to your seats

el músico
el mooseekoh
musician

el teatro
el tay-ahtroh
theater

el teatro de la ópera
el tay-ahtroh day lah ohperah
opera house

el club nocturno
el kloob noktoornoh
nightclub

el cantante
el kantantay
singer

el pianista
el pyaneestah
pianist

el cine
el theenay
movie theater

las palomitas
de maíz
*las palomeetas
day ma-eeth*
popcorn

el casino
el kaseenoh
casino

el ballet
el baleh
ballet

GALLERIES AND MUSEUMS

What are the opening hours?
¿Qué horario tiene?
kay ohraryoh tyenay

Are there guided tours in English?
¿Hay visitas guiadas en inglés?
ah-ee beeseetas gheeyadas en eenglais

When does the tour leave?
¿De dónde parte el recorrido?
day donday partay el rekorreedoh

How much does it cost?
¿Cuánto cuesta?
kwantoh kwestah

How long does it take?
¿Cuánto dura?
kwantoh doorah

Do you have an audio guide?
¿Tienen una guía en audio?
tyenen oonah gheeya en ah-oodyoh

Do you have a guidebook in English?
¿Tienen una guía en inglés?
tyenen oonah gheeya en eenglais

Is (flash) photography allowed?
¿Permiten hacer fotos (con flash)?
permeetain ahthair fotos (kon flash)

la estatua
lah estatwa
statue

el busto
el boostoh
bust

Can you direct me to...?	¿Puede indicarme el camino a...? *pweday eendeekarmay el kameenoh uh*
I'd really like to see...	Me gustaría ver... *may goostarya ber*
Who painted this?	¿Quién ha pintado esto? *kyen ah peentadoh estoh*
How old is it?	¿Cuántos años hace? *kwantos anyos ahthay*
Are there wheelchair ramps?	¿Hay rampas para sillas de ruedas? *ah-ee rampas parah seeyus day rwedas*
Is there an elevator?	¿Hay ascensor? *ah-ee asthensor*
Where are the restrooms?	¿Dónde están los aseos? *donday están los ahsaios*
I've lost my group	He perdido a mi grupo *eh perdeedoh uh mee groopoh*

la pintura
lah peentoorah
painting

el dibujo
el deeboohoh
drawing

el grabado
el grabadoh
engraving

el manuscrito
el manooscreetoh
manuscript

HOME ENTERTAINMENT

How do I...	¿Cómo se... *komoh say*
...turn on the television?	...enciende el televisor? *enthyenday el telebeesor*
...change channels?	...cambian los canales? *kambyan los kanalais*
...turn up the volume?	...le sube el volumen? *lay soobay el boloomain*
...turn down the volume?	...le baja el volumen? *lay bahah el boloomain*
Do you have satellite TV?	¿Tiene televisión por satélite? *tyenay telebeesyon por sateleetay*
Where can I buy...	¿Dónde se puede comprar... *donday say pweday komprar*
...a DVD?	...un DVD? *oon dayoobeday*
...a music CD?	...un CD de música? *oon thay day day mooseekah*

el televisor de pantalla ancha
el telebeesor day pantayah anchah
widescreen TV

el reproductor de DVD
el reprodooktor day dayoobeday
DVD player

el mando a distancia
el mandoh ah deestanthya
remote control

el videojuego
el beedaiohoo-aygoh
video game

la memoria USB
lah maimoreeah ooh aisay buy
USB flash drive

el portátil
el portateel
laptop

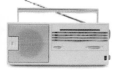

la radio
lah rahdyo
radio

el disco duro
el deeskoh dooroh
hard drive

el ratón
el raton
mouse

Can I use this to...	¿Puedo usar esto para... *pwedoh oosar estoh parah*
...go online?	...conectarme a Internet? *konektarmay uh internet*
Is it broadband/wifi?	¿Es banda ancha/wifi? *es bandah anchah/weefee*
How do I...	¿Cómo... *komoh*
...log on?	...inicio sesión? *eeneethyo sesyon*
...log out?	...cierro sesión? *thyerroh sesyon*
...reboot?	...reinicio? *reh-eeneethyo*

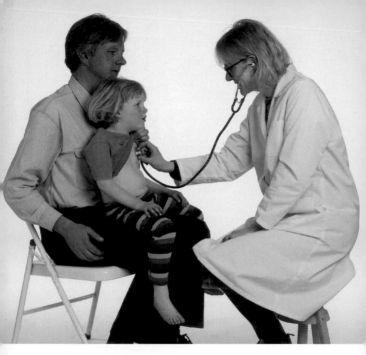

HEALTH

EU nationals receive free emergency medical care in Spain, provided they produce a European Health Insurance Card. Visitors from outside the EU should ensure that their health insurance covers them for medical treatment in Spain, or purchase special travel insurance. It is a good idea to familiarize yourself with a few basic phrases in case you need to visit a pharmacy or doctor.

I need a doctor	Necesito un médico *netheseetoh oon medeekoh*
I would like an appointment...	Quisiera que me dieran hora... *keesyeruh kay may deeyehran ohrah*
...as soon as possible	...lo antes posible *loh antais poseeblay*
...today	...para hoy *parah oi*
...tomorrow	...para mañana *parah manyanah*
It's very urgent	Es muy urgente *es mooy oorhentay*
I have a European Health Insurance Card	Tengo la tarjeta del seguro europeo *taingoh lah tarhetah dail segooroh eh-ooropuioh*
I have health insurance	Tengo seguro médico *taingoh segooroh medeekoh*
May I have a receipt?	¿Me puede dar un comprobante? *may pweday dar oon komprobantay*
Where is the nearest...	¿Dónde está... *donday estah*
...pharmacy?	...la farmacia más cercana? *lah farmatheeya mas therkanah*
...doctor's office?	...el ambulatorio más cercano? *el amboolatoryo mas therkanoh*
...hospital?	...el hospital más cercano? *el ospeetal mas therkanoh*
...dentist?	...el dentista más cercano? *el denteestah mas therkanoh*

AT THE PHARMACY

What can I take for...?	¿Qué me puedo tomar para...? *kay may pwedoh tomar parah*
How many should I take?	¿Cuántos tengo que tomar? *Kwantos taingoh kay tomar*
Is it safe for children?	¿Se les puede dar a los niños? *say lais pweday dar ah los neenyos*
Are there side effects?	¿Tiene efectos secundarios? *tyenay aifektos sekoondaryos*
Do you have that...	¿Lo tiene en... *loh tyenay en*
...in tablet form?	...pastillas? *pasteeyas*
...in capsule form?	...en cápsulas? *en kapsoolas*
I'm allergic to...	Soy alérgico a... *soy alerheekoh ah*
I'm already taking...	Ya estoy tomando... *ya estoy tomandoh*
Do I need a prescription?	¿Necesito una receta? *netheseetoh oonah rethetah*

YOU MAY HEAR...

Tómese esto...veces al día
tomesay estoh...bethays al deeyah
Take this...times a day

Con la comida
kon lah komeedah
With food

la venda
luh bendah
bandage

la tirita
lah teereetah
adhesive
bandage

las cápsulas
las kapsoolas
capsules

las pastillas
las pasteeyas
pills

la pomada
lah pohmadah
ointment

el supositorio
el sooposeetoryo
suppositories

las gotas
las gohtas
drops

el inhalador
el eenaladar
inhaler

el aerosol
el aehrosol
spray

el jarabe
el harabay
syrup

THE HUMAN BODY

I have hurt my...   Me he hecho daño en el...
may hay aicho danyo en el

I have cut my...   Me he cortado el...
may hay kortadoh el

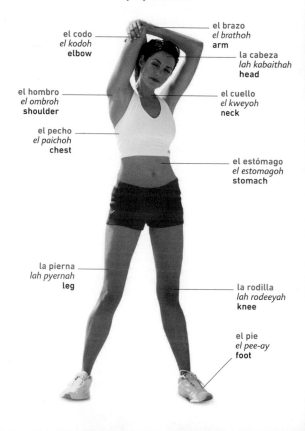

el codo
el kodoh
elbow

el brazo
el brathoh
arm

la cabeza
lah kabaithah
head

el hombro
el ombroh
shoulder

el cuello
el kweyoh
neck

el pecho
el paichoh
chest

el estómago
el estomagoh
stomach

la pierna
lah pyernah
leg

la rodilla
lah rodeeyah
knee

el pie
el pee-ay
foot

FACE

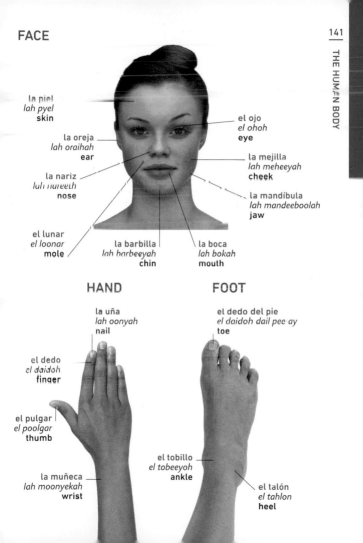

la piel
lah pyel
skin

el ojo
el ohoh
eye

la oreja
lah oraihah
ear

la mejilla
lah meheeyah
cheek

la nariz
lah nareeth
nose

la mandíbula
lah mandeeboolah
jaw

el lunar
el loonar
mole

la barbilla
lah barbeeyah
chin

la boca
lah bokah
mouth

HAND

FOOT

la uña
lah oonyah
nail

el dedo del pie
el daidoh dail pee-ay
toe

el dedo
el daidoh
finger

el pulgar
el poolgar
thumb

la muñeca
lah moonyekah
wrist

el tobillo
el tobeeyoh
ankle

el talón
el tahlon
heel

FEELING SICK

I don't feel well	No me encuentro bien *noh may enkwentroh byen*
I feel sick	Estoy enfermo *estoy ainfermoh*
I have...	Tengo... *taingoh*
...an ear ache	...dolor de oídos *dolor day o-eedos*
...a stomach ache	...dolor de estómago *dolor day estomagoh*
...a sore throat	...dolor de garganta *dolor day gargantah*
...a temperature	...fiebre *feeyebreh*
...hayfever	...alergia al polen *alerhyah al pohlain*
...constipation	...estreñimiento *estrenyeemyentoh*
...diarroea	...diarrea *dyarraiah*
...toothache	...dolor de muelas *dolor day moo-ailas*
I've been stung by...	Me ha picado... *may ah peekadoh*
...a bee/wasp	...una abeja/una avispa *oonah abehah/oonah abeespah*
...a jellyfish	...una medusa *oonah medoosah*
I've been bitten by...	Me ha mordido... *may ah mordeedoh*
...a dog	...un perro *oon perroh*

INJURIES

la mordedura
lah mordedoorah
bite

la picadura
lah peekadoorah
sting

la fractura
lah fraktoorah
fracture

el rasguño
el rasgoonyoh
graze

la astilla
lah asteeyah
splinter

la quemadura
lah kaimadoorah
burn

el corte
el kortay
cut

el cardenal
el kardainal
bruise

la quemadura de sol
lah kaimadoorah day sol
sunburn

el esguince
el esgheenthay
sprain

AT THE DOCTOR

I'm...   Estoy...
                            Estoy

...vomiting   ...vomitando
                            bomeetandoh

...bleeding   ...sangrando
                            sangrandoh

...dizzy   ...mareado/a
                            maraiadoh/ah

...feeling faint   ...desmayándome
                            daismayandomay

...pregnant   ...embarazada
                            embarathadah

...diabetic   ...diabético/a
                            deeyabeteekoh/ah

...epileptic   ...epiléptico/a
                            epeelepteekoh/ah

I have...   Tengo...
                            taingoh

...arthritis   ...artritis
                            artreetees

...a heart condition   ...una enfermedad cardíaca
                            oonah ainfermedad kardyakah

...high blood pressure   ...la presión alta
                            lah presyon altah

YOU MAY HEAR...

¿Qué le pasa?   ¿Dónde le duele?
kay lay pasah   *donday lay dweleh*
What's wrong?   **Where does
                            it hurt?**

ILLNESS

el resfriado
el resfreeyadoh
cold

la tos
lah tos
cough

el asma
el asmah
asthma

la gripe
lah greepay
the flu

el estornudo
el estornoodoh
sneeze

el calambre
el kalambray
stomach cramps

la náusea
lah naoosulu
nausea

el sarpullido
el sarpooyeedoh
rash

la hemorragia nasal
lah emorrahya nasal
nosebleed

el dolor de cabeza
el dolor day kabaithah
headache

AT THE HOSPITAL

Can you help me?	¿Puede ayudarme? *pweday ahyoodarmay*
I need...	Necesito... *netheseetoh*
...a doctor	...un médico *oon medeekoh*
...a nurse	...una enfermera *oonah ainfermerah*
Where is...	¿Dónde está... *donday estah*
...the emergency room?	...urgencias? *oorhenthyas*
...the children's ward?	...la sala de pediatría? *lah salah day paidyatrya*
...the X-ray department?	...el departamento de las radiografías? *el daipartamentoh day las radyografyas*
...the waiting room?	...la sala de urgencias? *lah salah day oorhenthyas*

la inyección
lah eenjekthyon
injection

la radiografía
lah radyografya
X-ray

el análisis de sangre
el analeesees day sangray
blood test

el escáner
el eskanair
scan

...the intensive care unit?	...la unidad de cuidados intensivos? *lah ooneedad day kweedados eentenseebos*
...the elevator/stairs?	...el ascensor/las escaleras? *el asthensor/las eskaleras*
I think I've broken...	Creo que me he roto... *krai-oh kay may eh rotoh*
Do I need...	¿Necesito... *netheseetoh*
...an injection?	...una inyección? *oonah eenjekthyon*
...antibiotics?	...antibióticos? *anteebeeyoteekos*
...an operation?	...una operación? *oonah ohperathyon*
Will it hurt?	¿Me dolerá? *may dolerah*
How long will it take?	¿Cuánto durará? *kwantoh doorarah*

el boca a boca
el bokah ah bokah
resuscitation

la silla de ruedas
lah seeyah day rwedas
wheelchair

la tablilla
lah tableeyah
splint

el vendaje
el bendahay
dressing

EMERGENCIES

In an emergency, you should dial the pan-European number 112 for an ambulance (*una ambulancia*), the fire department (*los bomberos*), and the police (*la policía*). You can use this number from both landlines and cell phones. If you are the victim of a crime or you lose your passport, money, or other possessions, you should report the incident to the police without delay.

IN AN EMERGENCY

Help!	**¡Socorro!** *sokorroh*
Please go away!	**¡Váyase!** *byasay*
Let go!	**¡Suélteme!** *sweltemay*
Stop! Thief!	**¡Alto! ¡Al ladrón!** *altoh al ladron*
Call the police!	**¡Llamen a la policía!** *yamain ah lah politheeya*
Get a doctor!	**¡Llamen a un médico!** *yamain ah oon medeekoh*
I need...	**Necesito...** *netheseetoh*
...the police	**...a la policía** *ah lah politheeya*
...the fire department	**...a los bomberos** *ah los bomberos*
...an ambulance	**...una ambulancia** *oonah amboolanthya*
It's very urgent	**Es muy urgente** *es mooy oorhentuy*
Where is...	**¿Dónde está...** *donday estah*
...the American/British embassy?	**...la embajada de los Estados Unidos/británica?** *lah embahadah day los estardos ooneedos/breetaneekah*
...the police station?	**...la comisaría?** *lah komeesarya*
...the hospital?	**...el hospital?** *el ospeetal*

ACCIDENTS

I need to make a telephone call	Tengo que llamar por teléfono *taingoh kay yamar por telefonoh*
I'd like to report an accident	Quiero informar de un accidente *kyeroh eenformar day oon aktheedentay*
I've crashed my car	He chocado con el coche *eh chokadoh kon el kochay*
The registration number is...	La matrícula es... *lah matreekoolah es*
I'm at...	Estoy en... *estoy en*
Please come quickly!	¡Vengan rápido, por favor! *baingan rapeedoh por fabor*
Someone's injured	Hay heridos *ah-ee ehreedos*
Someone's been knocked down	Ha habido un atropello *ah abeedoh oon atropeyoh*
There's a fire at...	Hay un incendio en... *ah-ee oon eenthendyo en*
Someone is trapped in the building	Hay alguien atrapado en el edificio *ah-ee alghyen atrapadoh en el edeefeethyo*

YOU MAY HEAR...

¿Qué servicio precisa?
kay serbeethyo praytheesah
Which service do you require?

¿Qué ha pasado?
kay ah pasadoh
What happened?

EMERGENCY SERVICES

la boca de riego
lah bokah day reeyegoh
fire hydrant

los bomberos
los bomberos
firefighters

el extintor
el eksteentor
fire extinguisher

el coche patrulla
el kochay patrooyah
police car

las esposas
las aisposas
handcuffs

la alarma de incendios
lah alarmah day eenthendyos
fire alarm

el policía
el politheeya
police officer

la ambulancia
lah amboolanthya
ambulance

el camión de bomberos
el kamyon day bomberos
fire engine

POLICE AND CRIME

I want to report a crime	**Quiero poner una denuncia** *kyeroh ponair oonah denoonthya*
I've been...	**Me han...** *may ahn*
...robbed	**...asaltado** *asaltadoh*
...attacked	**...atacado** *atakadoh*
...mugged	**...atracado** *atrakadoh*
...raped	**...violado** *beeyoladoh*
...burgled	**...robado** *robadoh*
Someone has stolen...	**Me han robado...** *may ahn robadoh*
...my car	**...el coche** *el kochay*
...my money	**...el dinero** *el deeneroh*
...my passport	**...el pasaporte** *el pasaportay*

YOU MAY HEAR...

¿Cuándo ha pasado?
kwandoh ah pasadoh
When did it happen?

¿Qué aspecto tenía?
kay aspektoh tainya
What did he look like?

¿Hay testigos?
ah-ee testeego
Was there a witness?

I'd like to speak to...	Quiero hablar con...
	kyeroh ahblar kon
...a senior officer	...un superior
	oon sooperyor
...a policewoman	...una mujer policía
	oonah moohair politheeya
I need...	Necesito...
	netheseetoh
...a lawyer	...un abogado
	oon abogadoh
...an interpreter	...un intérprete
	oon eenterpretay
...to make a phone call	...hacer una llamada
	ahthair oonah yamadah
I'm very sorry, officer	Lo siento mucho, agente
	loh syentoh moochoh ahentay
Here is...	Aquí tiene...
	ahkee tyenay
...my driver's license	...mi carné de conducir
	mee karnay day kondootheer
...my insurance	...mi seguro
	mee segooroh
How much is the fine?	¿Cuánto es la multa?
	kwantoh es lah mooltah

YOU MAY HEAR...

Su carné de conducir, por favor
soo karnay day kondootheer, por fabor
Your license, please

Sus papeles, por favor
soos papailays por fabor
Your papers, please

AT THE GARAGE

Where is the nearest garage?
¿Dónde está el taller mecánico más cercano?
donday estah el tayair mekaneekoh mas therkanoh

Can you do repairs?
¿Hace reparaciones?
ahthay rayparathyones

I need...
Necesito...
netheseetoh

...a new tire
...que cambie el neumático
kay kambeeyay el nayoomateekoha

...a new exhaust
...que cambie el tubo de escape
kay kambeeyay el tooboh day eskapay

...a new windshield
...que cambie el parabrisas
kay kambeeyay el parabreesas

...a new headlight
...que cambie la bombilla
kay kambeeyay lah bombeeyah

...wiper blades
...limpiaparabrisas
leempyaparabreesas

Do you have one in stock?
¿Tiene alguno aquí?
tyenay algoonoh ahkee

Can you replace this?
¿Puede cambiar esto?
pweday kambyar estoh

The...is not working
El...no funciona
el...noh foonthyonah

There is something wrong with the engine
Le pasa algo al motor
lay pasah algoh al mohtor

How long will it take?
¿Cuánto tardará?
kwantoh tardarah

When will it be ready?
¿Cuándo estará listo?
kwandoh estarah leestoh

How much will it cost?
¿Cuánto costará?
kwantoh kostarah

CAR BREAKDOWN

My car has broken down
Se me ha averiado el coche
say may ah aberyadoh el kochay

Please can you help me?
¿Puede ayudarme, por favor?
pweday ahyoodarmuy por fabor

Please come to...
Por favor, venga a...
por fabor bengah ah

I have a flat tire
Se me ha pinchado una rueda
say may ah peenchadoh oonah rwedah

Can you help change the wheel?
¿Puede ayudarme a cambiar la rueda?
pweday ahyoodarmuy ah kambeeyar lah rwedah

I need a new tire
Necesito un neumático nuevo
netheseetoh oon nayoomateekoh noo-eboh

My car won't start
El coche no arranca
el kochay noh arankah

The engine is overheating
El motor se ha recalentado
el mohtor say ah rekalentadoh

Can you fix it?
¿Puede arreglarlo?
pweday areglarloh

YOU MAY HEAR...

¿Necesita ayuda?
netheseetah ahyoodah
Do you need any help?

¿Lleva rueda de repuesto?
yaybah rwedah day repwestoh
Do you have a spare tire?

LOST PROPERTY

I've lost...
He perdido...
eh perdeedoh

...my money
...el dinero
el deeneroh

...my keys
...las llaves
las yabais

...my glasses
...las gafas
las gafas

My luggage is missing
Se ha perdido mi equipaje
say ah perdeedoh mee ekeepahay

Has it turned up yet?
¿Ha aparecido ya?
ah ahparetheedoh yah

My suitcase has been damaged
Mi maleta está estropeada
mee maletah estah aistropeadah

la cartera
lah karterah
wallet

el pasaporte
el pasaportay
passport

la tarjeta de crédito
lah tarhetah day kredeetoh
credit card

el monedero
el monaideroh
change purse

la cámara
lah kamarah
camera

el teléfono
inteligente
*el telefonoh
eentaileehaintay*
smartphone

el maletín
el malaiteen
briefcase

el bolso
el bolsoh
handbag

la maleta
la malaitah
suitcase

I need to phone my insurance company	Tengo que llamar a mi compañía de seguros *taingoh kay yamar ah mee kompanyeeah day segooros*
Can I put a stop on my credit cards?	¿Puedo invalidar mis tarjetas de crédito? *pwedoh eenbaleedar mees turhetas day kredectoh*
My name is...	Me llamo... *may yamoh*
My policy number is...	El número de mi póliza es... *el noomeroh day mee poleethah es*
My address is...	Mi dirección es... *mee deerekthyon es*
My contact number is...	Mi número de contacto es... *mee noomeroh day kontaktoh es*
My email address is...	Mi dirección de email es... *mee deerekthyon day eemaeel es*

MENU GUIDE

This guide lists the most common terms you may encounter on Spanish menus or when shopping for food. If you can't find an exact phrase, then try looking up its component parts.

A

aceitunas *olives*
acelgas *spinach beet*
achicoria *chicory*
aguacate *avocado*
ahumados *smoked*
agua mineral *mineral water*
ajo *garlic*
al ajillo *with garlic*
a la plancha *grilled*
albaricoques *apricots*
albóndigas *meatballs*
alcachofas *artichokes*
alcaparras *capers*
al horno *baked*
allioli *garlic mayonnaise*
almejas *clams*
almejas a la marinera *clams stewed in wine and parsley*
almejas naturales *live clams*
almendras *almonds*
almíbar *syrup*
alubias *beans*
ancas de rana *frogs' legs*
anchoas *anchovies*
anguila *eel*
angulas *baby eels*
arenque *herring*
arroz a la cubana *rice with fried eggs and banana fritters*
arroz a la valenciana *rice with seafood*
arroz con leche *rice pudding*
asados *roast meat*
atún *tuna*
azúcar *sugar*

B

bacalao a la vizcaína *cod with ham, peppers, chilies*
bacalao al pil pil *cod served with chilies and garlic*
batido *milk shake*
bebidas *drinks*
berenjenas *egg plant*
besugo al horno *baked red bream*
bistec de ternera *veal steak*
bonito fish *similar to tuna*
boquerones fritos *fried fresh anchovies*
brazo de gitano *swiss roll*
brocheta de riñones *kidney kebabs*
buñuelos *fried pastries*
butifarra *Catalan sausage*

C

cabrito asado *roast kid*
cacahuetes *peanuts*
cachelada *pork stew with eggs, tomato, and onion*
café *coffee*
café con leche *coffee with steamed milk*
calabacines *zucchini*
calabaza *pumpkin*

calamares a la romana
  squid rings in batter
calamares en su tinta *squid
  cooked in their ink*
caldeirada *fish soup*
caldereta gallega
  vegetable stew
caldo de... ...*soup*
caldo de gallina *chicken soup*
caldo de pescado *clear fish soup*
caldo gallego *vegetable soup*
caldo guanche *potato, onion, and
  tomato soup*
callos a la madrileña *tripe
  cooked with chilies*
camarones *shrimps*
canela *cinnamon*
cangrejos *crabs*
caracoles *snails*
caramelos *sweets*
carnes *meats*
castañas *chestnuts*
cebolla *onion*
cebolletas *scallions*
centollo *spider crab*
cerdo *pork*
cerezas *cherries*
cerveza *beer*
cesta de frutas *selection
  of fresh fruit*
champiñones *mushrooms*
chanquetes *fish (similar
  to whitebait)*
chipirones *baby squid*
chipirones en su tinta *squid
  cooked in their ink*
chocos *cuttlefish*
chorizo *spicy sausage*
chuleta de buey *beef chop*
chuleta de cerdo *pork chop*
chuleta de cerdo empanada
  breaded pork chop
chuleta de cordero *lamb chop*

chuleta de cordero empanada
  breaded lamb chop
chuleta de ternera *veal chop*
chuleta de ternera empanada
  breaded veal chop
chuletas de lomo ahumado
  smoked pork chops
chuletitas de cordero *small
  lamb chops*
chuletón *large chop*
chuletón de buey *large beef chop*
churros *deep-fried pastry strips*
cigalas *Scottish langoustines*
cigalas cocidas *boiled Scottish
  langoustines*
ciruelas *plums*
ciruelas pasas *prunes*
cochinillo asado *roast
  suckling pig*
cocido *meat, chickpea,
  and vegetable stew*
cocochas (de merluza)
  hake stew
cóctel de bogavante
  lobster cocktail
cóctel de gambas *shrimp cocktail*
cóctel de langostinos *king
  prawn cocktail*
cóctel de mariscos
  seafood cocktail
codornices *quail*
codornices escabechadas
  marinated quail
codornices estofadas
  braised quail
col *cabbage*
coles de Bruselas
  Brussels sprouts
coliflor *cauliflower*
coñac *brandy*
conejo *rabbit*
conejo encebollado *rabbit
  with onions*

congrio *conger eel*
consomé con yema *consommé with egg yolk*
consomé de ave *fowl consommé*
contra de ternera con guisantes *veal stew with peas*
contrafilete de ternera *veal fillet*
copa *glass (of wine)*
copa de helado *ice cream, assorted flavors*
cordero asado *roast lamb*
cordero chilindrón *lamb stew with onion, tomato, peppers, and eggs*
costillas de cerdo *pork ribs*
crema catalana *crème brûlée*
cremada *dessert made with egg, sugar, and milk*
crema de... *cream of...soup*
crema de legumbres *cream of vegetable soup*
crepe imperial *crepe suzette*
criadillas de tierra *truffles*
crocante *ice cream with chopped nuts*
croquetas *croquettes*
cuajada *curds*

D, E

dátiles *dates*
embutidos *sausages*
embutidos de la tierra *local sausages*
empanada gallega *fish pie*
empanada santiaguesa *fish pie*
empanadillas *small pies*
endivia *endive*
en escabeche *marinated*
ensalada *salad*
ensalada de arenque *fish salad*
ensalada ilustrada *mixed salad*
ensalada mixta *mixed salad*

ensalada *simple green salad*
ensaladilla rusa *Russian salad (potatoes, carrots, peas, and other vegetables in mayonnaise)*
entrecot a la parrilla *grilled entrecôte*
entremeses *hors d'oeuvres starters*
escalope a la milanesa *breaded veal with cheese*
escalope a la parrilla *broiled veal*
escalope a la plancha *broiled veal*
escalope de lomo de cerdo *escalope of pork fillet*
escalope de ternera *veal escalope*
escalope empanado *breaded escalope*
escalopines al vino de Marsala *veal escalopes cooked in Marsala wine*
escalopines de ternera *veal escalopes*
espadín a la toledana *kebab*
espaguetis *spaghetti*
espárragos *asparagus*
espárragos trigueros *wild green asparagus*
espinacas *spinach*
espinazo de cerdo con patatas *stew of pork ribs with potatoes*
estofado *braised; stew*
estragón *tarragon*

F

fabada (asturiana) *bean stew with sausage*
faisán *pheasant*
faisán trufado *pheasant with truffles*
fiambres *cold meats*
fideos *thin pasta, noodles*
filete a la parrilla *grilled beef steak*

filete de cerdo *pork steak*
filete de ternera *veal steak*
flan *crème caramel*
frambuesas *raspberries*
fresas *strawberries*
fritos *fried*
fruta *fruit*

G

gallina en pepitoria *chicken stew with peppers*
gambas *prawns*
gambas cocidas *boiled prawns*
gambas en gabardina *prawns in batter*
gambas rebozadas *prawns in batter*
garbanzos *chickpeas*
garbanzos a la catalana *chickpeas with sausage, boiled eggs, and pine nuts*
gazpacho andaluz *cold tomato soup*
gelatina de... *...jelly*
gratén de... *...au gratin (baked in a cream and cheese sauce)*
granizado *crushed ice drink*
gratinada/o *au gratin*
grelo *turnip*
grillado *grilled*
guisantes *peas*
guisantes salteados *sautéed peas*

H

habas *fava beans*
habichuelas *white beans*
helado *ice cream*
helado de vainilla *vanilla ice cream*
helado de turrón *nougat ice cream*

hígado *liver*
hígado de ternera *calves' liver*
hígado estofado *braised liver*
higos con miel y nueces *figs with honey and nuts*
higos secos *dried figs*
horchata (de chufas) *cold drink made from tiger nuts*
huevo hilado *egg yolk garnish*
huevos *eggs*
huevos a la flamenca *fried eggs with ham, tomato, and vegetables*
huevos cocidos *hard-boiled eggs*
huevos con patatas fritas *fried eggs and chips*
huevos con picadillo *eggs with ground meat*
huevos duros *hard-boiled eggs*
huevos escalfados *poached eggs*
huevos pasados por agua *soft-boiled eggs*
huevos revueltos *scrambled eggs*

J

jamón *ham*
jamón con huevo hilado *ham with egg yolk garnish*
jamón serrano *cured ham*
jarra de vino *wine jug*
jerez *sherry*
jeta *pigs' cheeks*
judías verdes *green beans*
judías verdes a la española *bean stew*
judías verdes al natural *plain green beans*
jugo de... *...juice*

L

langosta *lobster*
langosta a la americana
lobster with brandy and garlic
langosta a la catalana *lobster
with mushrooms and ham in
white sauce*
langosta fría con mayonesa
cold lobster with mayonnaise
langostinos *king prawns*
langostinos dos salsas
*king prawns cooked in
two sauces*
laurel *bay leaves*
leche *milk*
leche frita *pudding made from
milk and eggs*
leche merengada *cold milk
with meringue*
lechuga *lettuce*
lengua de buey *ox tongue*
lengua de cordero
lamb's tongue
lenguado a la romana *sole
in batter*
lenguado meuniere *floured sole
fried in butter*
lentejas *lentils*
lentejas aliñadas *lentils
in vinaigrette dressing*
licores *spirits, liqueurs*
liebre estofada *stewed hare*
lima *lime*
limón *lemon*
lombarda *red cabbage*
lomo curado *pork sausage*
lonchas de jamón *sliced,
cured ham*
longaniza *cooked
Spanish sausage*
lubina *sea bass*
lubina a la marinera *sea bass
in a parsley sauce*

M

macedonia de fruta *fruit salad*
mahonesa or mayonesa
mayonnaise
Málaga *a sweet wine*
mandarinas *tangerines*
manitas de cordero *lamb shank*
manos de cerdo *pigs' feet*
manos de cerdo a la parrilla
grilled pigs' feet
mantecadas *small sponge cakes*
mantequilla *butter*
manzanas *apples*
mariscada *cold mixed shellfish*
mariscos del día *fresh shellfish*
mariscos del tiempo
seasonal shellfish
medallones *steaks*
media de agua *half bottle
of mineral water*
mejillones *mussels*
mejillones a la marinera
mussels in a wine sauce
melocotón *peach*
melón *melon*
menestra de legumbres
vegetable stew
menú de la casa *set menu*
menú del día *set menu*
merluza *hake*
merluza a la cazuela
stewed hake
merluza al ajo arriero *hake
with garlic and chillies*
merluza a la riojana *hake
with chilies*
merluza a la romana *hake
steaks in batter*
merluza a la vasca *hake in
a garlic sauce*
merluza en salsa *hake in sauce*
merluza en salsa verde *hake
in parsley and wine sauce*

merluza fría *cold hake*
merluza frita *fried hake*
mermelada *jam*
mero *grouper (fish)*
mero en salsa verde *grouper in garlic and parsley sauce*
mollejas de ternera fritas *fried sweetbreads*
morcilla *blood sausage*
morcilla de carnero *mutton blood sausage*
morros de cerdo *pigs' cheeks*
morros de vaca *cows' cheeks*
mortadela *salami-type sausage*
morteruelo *kind of pâté*

N, O

nabo *turnip*
naranjas *oranges*
nata *cream*
natillas *cold custard*
níscalos *wild mushrooms*
nueces *walnuts*
orejas de cerdo *pigs' ears*

P

paella *fried rice with seafood and/or meat*
paella castellana *meat paella*
paella valenciana *vegetables, snail, rabbit, and chicken paella*
paleta de cordero lechal *shoulder of lamb*
pan *bread*
panaché de verduras *vegetable stew*
panceta *bacon*
parrillada de caza *mixed grilled game*
parrillada de mariscos *mixed grilled shellfish*
pasas *raisins*
pastel de ternera *veal pie*

pasteles *cakes*
patatas a la pescadora *potatoes with fish*
patatas asadas *baked potatoes*
patatas bravas *potatoes in spicy sauce*
patatas fritas *French fries*
patitos rellenos *stuffed duckling*
pato a la naranja *duck in orange sauce*
pavo *turkey*
pavo trufado *turkey stuffed with truffles*
pecho de ternera *breast of veal*
pechuga de pollo *breast of chicken*
pepinillos *gherkins*
pepino *cucumber*
peras *pears*
percebes *edible barnacle*
perdices a la campesina *partridges with vegetables*
perdices a la manchega *partridges in red wine, garlic, herbs, and pepper*
perdices escabechadas *marinated partridges*
perejil *parsley*
perritos calientes *hot dogs*
pescaditos fritos *fried fish*
pestiños *sugared pastries flavored with aniseed*
pez espada *swordfish*
picadillo de ternera *minced veal*
pimienta negra *pepper*
pimientos *peppers*
pimientos a la riojana *baked red peppers fried in oil and garlic*
pimientos morrones *type of bell pepper*
pimientos verdes *green peppers*
piña al gratín *pineapple au gratin*

piña fresca *fresh pineapple*
pinchitos/pinchos *kebabs,*
snacks served in bars
pinchos morunos *pork kebabs*
piñones *pine nuts*
pisto *ratatouille*
pisto manchego *vegetable*
marrow with onion and tomato
plátanos *bananas*
plátanos flameados
flambéed bananas
pollo *chicken*
pollo a la riojana *chicken with*
peppers and chilies
pollo al ajillo *fried chicken*
with garlic
pollo asado *roast chicken*
pollo braseado *braised chicken*
pollo en cacerola *chicken casserole*
pollo en pepitoria *chicken*
in wine with saffron, garlic,
and almonds
pollos tomateros con zanahorias
young chicken with carrots
pomelo *grapefruit*
potaje castellano *thick broth*
potaje de... *...stew*
puchero canario *casserole of meat,*
chickpeas, and corn
pulpitos con cebolla
baby octopus with onions
pulpo *octopus*
puré de patatas *mashed potatoes,*
potato purée
purrusalda *cod with leeks*
and potatoes

Q

queso con membrillo *cheese*
with quince jelly
queso de bola *Dutch cheese*
queso de Burgos *soft*
white cheese

queso del país *local cheese*
queso de oveja *sheep's cheese*
queso gallego *creamy cheese*
Queso manchego *hard,*
strong cheese
quisquillas *shrimps*

R

rábanos *radishes*
ragú de ternera *veal ragoût*
rape a la americana
monkfish with brandy and herbs
rape a la cazuela *stewed monkfish*
raya *skate*
rebozado *in batter*
redondo al horno *roast fillet*
of beef
rellenos *stuffed*
remolacha *beet*
repollo *cabbage*
repostería de la casa *cakes*
that are baked on the premises
requesón *cream cheese,*
cottage cheese
revuelto de... *scrambled*
eggs with...
revuelto de ajos tiernos *scrambled*
eggs with spring garlic
revuelto de trigueros *scrambled*
eggs with asparagus
revuelto mixto *scrambled*
eggs with mixed vegetables
riñones *kidneys*
rodaballo *turbot (fish)*
romero *rosemary*
ron *rum*
roscas *sweet pastries*

S

sal *salt*
salchichas *sausages*
salchichas de Frankfurt *hot*
dog sausages

salchichón *sausage similar to salami*

salmón ahumado *smoked salmon*

salmonetes *red mullet*

salmonetes en papillote *red mullet cooked in foil*

salmón frío *cold salmon*

salmorejo *sauce of bread, tomatoes, oil, vinegar, and garlic*

salpicón de mariscos *shellfish in vinaigrette*

salsa *sauce*

salsa bechamel *white sauce*

salsa holandesa *hollandaise sauce*

sandía *watermelon*

sardinas a la brasa *barbecued sardines*

seco *dry*

semidulce *medium-sweet*

sesos *brains*

sesos a la romana *fried brains in butter*

sesos rebozados *brains in batter*

setas *mushrooms*

sidra *cider*

sobreasada *sausage with cayenne pepper*

solomillo *fillet steak*

solomillo con patatas *fillet steak with fries*

solomillo de ternera *fillet of veal*

solomillo de vaca *fillet of beef*

solomillo frío *cold roast beef*

sopa *soup*

sopa castellana *vegetable soup*

sopa de almendras *almond soup*

sopa de cola de buey *oxtail soup*

sopa de gallina *chicken soup*

sopa del día *soup of the day*

sopa de legumbres *vegetable soup*

sopa de marisco *fish and shellfish soup*

sopa de rabo de buey *oxtail soup*

sopa mallorquina *soup of tomato, meat, and eggs*

sopa sevillana *fish and mayonnaise soup*

soufflé de fresones *strawberry soufflé*

T

tallarines *noodles*

tallarines a la italiana *tagliatelle*

tarta *cake*

tarta de la casa *cake baked on the premises*

tarta de manzana *apple tart*

tencas *tench*

ternera asada *roast veal*

tocinillos de cielo *a very sweet crème caramel*

tomates *tomatoes*

tomillo *thyme*

torrijas *sweet pastries*

tortilla a la paisana *vegetable omelet*

tortilla a su gusto *omelet made to the customer's wishes*

tortilla de escabeche *fish omelet*

tortilla española *Spanish omelet with potato, onion, and garlic*

tortilla sacromonte *vegetable, brains, and sausage omelet*

tortillas variadas *assorted omelets*

tournedó *fillet steak*

trucha *trout*

trucha ahumada *smoked trout*

trucha escabechada
marinated trout
truchas a la marinera
trout in wine sauce
truchas molinera *trout meunière*
(floured trout fried in butter)
trufas *truffles*
turrón *nougat*

U, V

uvas *grapes*
verduras *vegetables*
vieiras *scallops*

**vino de mesa/blanco/rosado/
tinto** *table/white/rosé/red wine*

Z

zanahorias a la crema
creamed carrots
zarzuela de mariscos
seafood stew
**zarzuela de pescados
y mariscos** *fish and
shellfish stew*
zumo de... *...juice*

In this dictionary, nouns are given with their definite articles – el (generally masculine, but sometimes feminine; see the Spanish–English dictionary), la (feminine), los (masculine plural), and las (feminine plural). Spanish adjectives vary according to the gender and number of the word they describe. Most ending in "o" adopt an "a" ending in the feminine form; those ending in "e" usually stay the same.

A

a *un/a*
a little *un poco*
a lot *mucho*
about *más o menos*
about; around *alrededor de*
above *sobre*
accident *el accidente*
accident and emergency department
  las urgencias
accommodation *alojamiento*
account number *el número de la cuenta*
across *al otro lado*
activities *las actividades*
actor *el actor*
actress *la actriz*
adaptor *el adaptador*
add (verb) *sumar*
address *la dirección*
adhesive bandage *la tirita*
adhesive tape *la cinta adhesiva*
adult *adulto*
aerobics *el aeróbic*
after *después*
afternoon *la tarde*
aftersun *la crema para después del sol*
again *otra vez; de nuevo*
airbag *el airbag*
air-conditioning *el aire acondicionado*

aircraft *el avión*
airmail *por avión*
airplane *el avión*
airport *el aeropuerto*
air travel *los viajes en avión*
aisle *el pasillo*
aisle seat *el asiento de pasillo*
alarm clock
  el reloj despertador
alcoholic drinks
  las bebidas alcohólicas
all *todo*
allergic *alérgico*
allergy *la alergia*
almost *casi*
alone *solo*
along *por*
already *ya*
alright *bien*
altitude *la altitud*
always *siempre*
ambulance *la ambulancia*
amount *la cantidad*
and *y*
angry *enfadado*
animals *los animales*
ankle *el tobillo*
another; other *otro*
answer (verb) *contestar*
antibiotics *los antibióticos*
antiseptic *el desinfectante*
anything *algo*

apartment *el apartamento*
apartment building *el edificio*
appearance *el aspecto*
appetizer *el entrante*
applaud (verb) *aplaudir*
apple *la manzana*
apple juice *el zumo de manzana*
application *la aplicación*
appointment *la cita*
apricot *el albaricoque*
April *abril*
apron *el delantal*
arc *el arco*
arch *el arco*
architect *el/la arquitecto/a*
architecture *la arquitectura*
area *el área*
arm *el brazo*
arm rest *el apoyabrazos*
around *alrededor de*
arrangements *los arreglos*
arrivals *las llegadas*
arrivals hall *el vestíbulo de llegadas*
arrive (verb) *llegar*
art *el arte*
art gallery *la galería de arte*
arthritis *la artritis*
artificial sweetener *el edulcorante artificial*
artist *el/la artista; el/la pintor/a*
as (like) *como*
ashtray *el cenicero*
assistant *el/la ayudante*
asthma *el asma*
at *en*
athlete *el/la atleta*
ATM *el cajero automático*
attachment *el documento adjunto*
attack *el ataque*
attend (verb) *asistir*

attractions *las atracciones turísticas*
audience *el público*
audio guide *la guía en audio*
August *agosto*
aunt *la tía*
Australia *Australia*
automatic *automático*
automatic payment *la domiciliación bancaria*
automatic ticket machine *la máquina de billetes*
avenue *la avenida*
avocado *el aguacate*
awful *espantoso*

B

baby *el/la bebé*
baby changing room *el cuarto para cambiar a los bebés*
babysitting *hacer de canguro*
back *el respaldo*
back (body) *la espalda*
backpack *la mochila*
bad *malo*
badminton *el bádminton*
bag (luggage) *la bolsa*
bagel *la rosquilla*
baggage allowance *el equipaje permitido*
baggage claim *la recogida de equipajes*
baggage claim tag *la etiqueta de identificación de equipaje*
bake (verb) *cocer al horno*
baker *la panadería*
balcony *el balcón*
balcony (theater) *el gallinero*
ball *el balón; el ovillo; la pelota*
ballet *el ballet*
banana *el plátano*
bandage *el vendaje*
bank *el banco*

bank account *la cuenta bancaria*
bank charge *la comisión bancaria*
bank manager *el/la director/a del banco*
bank transfer *la transferencia bancaria*
bar *el bar*
bar snacks *los aperitivos*
barbecue *la barbacoa*
barber *el/la barbero/a*
bartender *el/la camarero/a*
baseball *el béisbol*
baseball glove *el guante de béisbol*
basement *el sótano*
basil *la albahaca*
basket *el cesto; la canasta*
basketball *el baloncesto*
bath *el baño*
bath robe *el albornoz*
bathroom *el cuarto de baño*
bath towel *la toalla de baño*
bathtub *la bañera*
battery *la pila*
be (verb) *estar; ser*
beach *la playa*
beach ball *la pelota de playa*
beach towel *la toalla de playa*
beach umbrella *la sombrilla*
beans *los granos*
bear *el/la oso/a*
beautiful *hermoso*
bed *la cama*
bed and breakfast *la habitación con desayuno incluido*
bed linen *la ropa de cama*
bedroom *el dormitorio*
bee *la abeja*
beef *la vaca*
beer *la cerveza*
beetle *el escarabajo*
beet *la remolacha*
before *antes de*

beginner *el/la principiante*
beginning *el principio*
behind *detrás de*
bell *el timbre*
below *debajo de*
belt *el cinturón*
bench *el banco*
beneath *por debajo de*
berry *la baya*
beside *al lado de*
better *mejor*
between *entre*
beyond *más allá de*
bicycle *la bicicleta*
bidet *el bidé*
big *grande*
bike rack *el aparcamiento para bicicletas*
bikini *el bikini*
bill (note) *la nota*
bird *el ave*
birth *el nacimiento*
birth certificate *la partida de nacimiento*
birthday *el cumpleaños*
bit *el bocado*
bite *el mordisco*
bitter *amargo*
black *negro*
blackberry *la mora*
black coffee *el café solo*
blackcurrant *la grosella negra*
black tea *el té negro*
blanket *la manta*
bleach *la lejía*
bleeding *la hemorragia*
blender *la licuadora*
blister *la ampolla*
block *la parada*
blonde *rubio*
blood *la sangre*
blood pressure *la tensión arterial*

blood test *el análisis de sangre*
blouse *la blusa*
blow dry (verb) *secar con el secador*
blow-dryer *el secador de pelo*
blue *azul*
blueberry *el arándano*
blush *el colorete*
board: on board *a bordo*
board (verb) *embarcar*
boarding gate *la puerta de embarque*
boarding pass *la tarjeta de embarque*
boat *el barco*
boat trip *la excursión en barco*
body *el cuerpo*
body lotion *la loción corporal*
boil (verb) *hervir*
book *el libro*
book (verb) *reservar*
book a flight (verb) *reservar un vuelo*
bookstore *la librería*
boot (footwear) *la bota*
bored *aburrido*
borrow (verb) *coger prestado*
bottle *la botella*
bottle opener *el abrebotellas*
bottled water *el agua embotellada*
bottom *el fondo*
bottom (body) *el trasero*
boutique *la boutique*
bowl *el cuenco*
bowling *los bolos*
box office *la taquilla*
boy *el chico*
boyfriend *el novio*
bracelet *la pulsera*
brain *el cerebro*
brake *el freno*
branch *la rama*
bread *el pan*

breakdown *la avería*
breakfast *el desayuno*
breakfast buffet *el buffet de desayuno*
breakfast cereals *los cereales*
brick *el ladrillo*
bridge *el empeine*
briefcase *el maletín*
briefs *los calzoncillos*
brioche *el brioche*
British *británico*
broccoli *el brócoli*
broil (verb) *asar a la parrilla*
brooch *el broche*
broom *la escoba*
brother *el hermano*
brown *marrón*
brown rice *el arroz integral*
browse (verb) *navegar*
bruise *el cardenal*
brunette *castaño*
brush *el cepillo*
bubblebath *el baño de burbujas*
bucket *el cubo*
buckle *la hebilla*
buffet *el buffet*
build (verb) *construir*
bulb *el bulbo*
bulletin board *el corcho*
bumper *el parachoques*
bun *el bollo*
bunch *el ramo*
buoy *la boya*
currency exchange *la oficina de cambio*
burger *la hamburguesa*
burgle (verb) *robar*
burn *la quemadura*
bus *el autobús*
bus driver *el/la conductor/a de autobús*
business *el negocio*

business class *la clase preferente*
bus station *la estación de autobuses*
bus stop *la parada de autobús*
bust *el busto*
bus ticket *el billete de autobús*
butcher *la carnicería*
butter *la mantequilla*
butternut squash *la calabaza butternut*
button *el botón*
buy (verb) *comprar*

C

cab *la cabina*
cabin (boat) *el camarote*
cable *el cable*
cable car *el teleférico*
cable television *la televisión por cable*
café *la cafetería*
cakes *los pasteles*
calculator *la calculadora*
calendar *el calendario*
call button *el timbre*
calm *tranquilo*
camera *la cámara*
camera bag *la funda de la cámara*
camisole *la camisola*
camper van *la caravana*
camper van site *el camping para caravanas*
camping kettle *el hervidor de agua para camping*
camping stove *el hornillo para camping*
camp (verb) *acampar*
campsite *el camping*
can (noun) *la lata*
can (verb) *poder*

can opener *el abrelatas*
Canada *Canadá*
candy *los caramelos*
canoe *la canoa*
cap *el gorro de baño*
capital *la capital*
cappuccino *el cappuccino*
capsule *la cápsula*
car *el coche*
car accident *el accidente de coche*
car crash *el accidente de coche*
card *la tarjeta*
cardboard *la cartulina*
cardigan *la rebeca*
cards *las cartas*
care for (verb) *encantar*
carnival *el carnaval*
carpet *la moqueta*
car rental *el alquiler de coches*
carrot *la zanahoria*
carry (verb) *llevar*
carry out *la comida para llevar*
car stereo *el equipo estéreo del coche*
cart *el carrito*
carton *el tetrabrik*
car wash *el lavadero de coches*
case *la funda*
cash (verb) *cobrar*
cash machine *el cajero automático*
cash register *la caja*
casino *el casino*
casserole dish *la olla*
castle *el castillo*
casual *sport*
cat *el gato*
catamaran *el catamarán*

catch (verb) *coger*
cathedral *la catedral*
cauliflower *la coliflor*
caution *precaución*
cave *la cueva*
CD *el CD*
ceiling *el techo*
celebration *la celebración*
cell phone *el móvil*
central heating
   la calefacción central
center *el centro*
cereal *los cereales*
chair *la silla*
chair lift *el telesilla*
champagne *el champán*
change (noun) *el cambio*
change (verb) *cambiar*
change purse *el monedero*
channel (TV) *el canal*
charge *el cargo*
charge (verb) *cobrar*
chart *la gráfica del paciente*
cheap *barato*
check (bill) *la cuenta*
checker *el/la cajero/a*
check in (airport) *facturar*
check-in desk *el mostrador
   de facturación*
check in (hotel) *registrarse*
check in (verb) *facturar*
checkout (supermarket)
   la caja
checkup *la revisión*
cheek *la mejilla*
cheers *salud*
cheese *el queso*
chef *el/la chef*
check *el cheque*
checkbook *el talonario
   de cheques*
check card *la tarjeta
   bancaria*

checking account *la cuenta
   corriente*
cherry *la cereza*
cherry tomato *el tomate cherry*
chest *el pecho*
chewing gum *el chicle*
chicken *el pollo*
chickpeas *los garbanzos*
child *el/la niño/a*
children *los niños*
chill *el resfriado*
chili *la guindilla*
chin *la barbilla*
chocolate *el bombón*
choke (verb) *ahogarse*
chop *la chuleta*
chorizo *el chorizo*
church *la iglesia*
cigar *el puro*
cigarette *el cigarrillo*
cilantro *el cilantro*
cinnamon *la canela*
circle *el círculo*
citrus fruit *los cítricos*
city *la ciudad*
clam *la almeja*
clean *limpio*
client *el cliente*
cliff *el acantilado*
clinic *la clínica*
clock *el reloj*
clock radio *la radio
   despertador*
close (verb) *cerrar*
closed *cerrado*
closet *el armario*
clothes *la ropa*
clothing *el equipo*
cloud *la nube*
cloudy *nublado*
club *el trébol*
coach *el autocar*
coast *la costa*

coaster *el posavasos*
coast guard *el guardacostas*
coat *el abrigo*
coat hanger *la percha*
cockroach *la cucaracha*
cocktail *el cóctel*
coconut *el coco*
cod *el bacalao*
coffee *el café*
coffee cup *la taza de café*
coffee machine *la máquina de café*
coffee table *la mesa de café*
coin *la moneda*
colander *el colador*
cold (adj) *frío*
cold (illness) *el resfriado*
collection *la recogida*
college *la enseñanza superior*
color *el color*
colored pencil *el lápiz de colores*
colors *los colores*
comb *el peine*
come (verb) *venir*
comforter *el edredón*
comic book *el tebeo*
company *la empresa*
compartment *el compartimento*
compass *la brújula*
complain (verb) *quejarse*
complaint *la denuncia*
computer *el ordenador*
concert *el concierto*
concourse *la sala de la estación*
conditioner *el suavizante*
condom *el condón*
confident *seguro de sí mismo*
confused *confundido*
connection *la conexión*
constipation *el estreñimiento*
construction site *la obra*
construction worker *el/la albañil*
consul *el/la cónsul*

consulate *el consulado*
consultation *la consulta*
contact lenses *las lentes de contacto*
contact number *el número de contacto*
container *el recipiente*
continent *el continente*
contraception *la anticoncepción*
cookie *la galleta*
cookie sheet *la bandeja de horno*
cooking *cocinar*
cooler *la nevera*
copy (verb) *fotocopiar*
coral reef *el arrecife de coral*
core *el corazón*
cork *el corcho*
corkscrew *el sacacorchos*
corn *el maíz*
corner *el córner*
correct *correcto*
cotton *el algodón*
cough *la tos*
cough medicine *el jarabe para la tos*
count (verb) *contar*
counter *la ficha*
country *el país*
couple *la pareja*
courier *el/la mensajero/a*
courses (meal) *los platos*
courtyard *el patio*
cousin *el/la primo/a*
cow *la vaca*
crab *el cangrejo*
cramp *el calambre*
cream cheese *el queso cremoso*
crease *la línea del bateador*

credit card *la tarjeta de crédito*
crêpes *las crêpes*
crib *la cuna*
crime *la delincuencia*
croissant *el croissant*
cross trainer *la bicicleta elíptica*
crushed *machacado*
crust *la corteza*
cry (verb) *llorar*
cucumber *el pepino*
cufflinks *los gemelos*
culture *la cultura*
cup *la taza*
curly *rizado*
curry *el curry*
curtain *el telón*
cushion *el cojín*
customer *el cliente*
customs *la aduana*
cut (verb) *cortar*
cutlery *los cubiertos*
cutting board *la tabla de cortar*
cycle (verb) *ir en bicicleta*
cycle lane *el carril de bicicletas*
cycling helmet *el casco de ciclista*

D

dairy *los lácteos*
dairy foods *los productos lácteos*
damaged *estropeado*
dance *la música de baile*
dance (verb) *bailar*
danger *peligro*
dark *moreno*
dashboard *el salpicadero*
daughter *la hija*
day *el día*
day planner *la agenda*

debit card *la tarjeta de débito*
December *diciembre*
deck chair *la hamaca*
deep-fried *frito con mucho aceite*
degrees *grados*
delayed *con retraso*
delicatessen *la charcutería*
delicious *delicioso*
delivery *el parto*
dentist *el dentista*
deodorant *el desodorante*
department *el departamento*
department store *los grandes almacenes*
departure board *el tablero de anuncios de salidas*
departure lounge *la sala de embarque*
departures *las salidas*
departures hall *el vestíbulo de salidas*
deposit *el depósito*
deposit (bank; verb) *ingresar*
desert *el desierto*
desk *el mostrador*
dessert *el postre*
dessert spoon *la cuchara de postre*
destination *el destino*
detergent *el detergente*
develop (a film) *revelar*
diabetic *diabético*
dial (verb) *marcar*
diaper *el pañal*
diarrhea *la diarrea*
dictionary *el diccionario*
diesel *diésel*
difficult *difícil*
digital camera *la cámara digital*
digital radio *la radio digital*
dining car *el vagón restaurante*
dining room *el comedor*

dinner *la cena*
directions *las direcciones*
dirty *sucio*
disabled parking *el aparcamiento para minusválidos*
disabled person *la persona minusválida*
discuss (verb) *discutir*
disembark (verb) *desembarcar*
dish *el plato*
dishes *la vajilla*
dishwasher *el friegaplatos*
distance *la distancia*
district *el distrito*
dive (verb) *tirarse*
divorced *divorciado*
do (verb) *hacer*
doctor *el/la médico/a*
doctor's office *la consulta del médico*
dog *el/la perro/a*
doll *la muñeca*
dolphin *el delfín*
don't *no*
door *la puerta*
doorbell *el timbre*
dosage *la dosis*
double bed *la cama de matrimonio*
double room *la habitación doble*
down *abajo*
download (verb) *bajar*
drain *el sumidero*
draw (verb) *dibujar*
drawer *el cajón*
drawing *el dibujo*
dress *el vestido*
dressing *el aliño*
drink (noun) *la bebida*
drink (verb) *beber*
drinks *las bebidas*
drive (verb) *conducir*

driver *el/la conductor/a*
driver's license *el carné de conducir*
drugstore *la farmacia*
dry *seco*
duck *el pato*
duffel bag *la bolsa de viaje*
during *durante*
dust pan *el recogedor*
duty-free store *la tienda libre de impuestos*
DVD *el DVD*
DVD player *el reproductor de DVD*

E

each *cada*
ear *la oreja*
early *temprano*
earring *el pendiente*
earthquake *el terremoto*
east *el este*
easy *fácil*
eat (verb) *comer*
eat-in *para comer en el local*
eating out *comer fuera*
egg *el óvulo*
eggplant *la berenjena*
elbow *el codo*
electric razor *la maquinilla eléctrica*
electrician *el/la electricista*
electricity *la electricidad*
elevator *el ascensor*
email address *la dirección de email*
embarrassed *avergonzado*
embassy *la embajada*
emergency *la urgencia*
emergency exit *la salida de emergencia*

emergency room *la sala de urgencias*
emergency services *los servicios de urgencia*
emigrate (verb) *emigrar*
empty *vacío*
end *el final*
engaged/busy *comunicando*
engine *el motor*
English *inglés*
engraving *el grabado*
enjoy (verb) *disfrutar*
enough *bastante*
entrance *la entrada*
entrance ramp *la vía de acceso*
envelope *el sobre*
epileptic *epiléptico*
equipment *el equipamiento*
espresso *el café solo*
euro *el euro*
evening *la noche*
evening dress *el traje de noche*
evening meal *la cena*
evening menu *el menú de la cena*
events *las modalidades*
every *cada*
exactly *exactamente*
examine (verb) *examinar*
exchange rate *el cambio*
excited *entusiasmado*
excursion *la excursión*
excuse me *perdone*
exercise bike *la bicicleta estática*
exhaust (car) *el tubo de escape*
exhibition *la exposición*
exit *la salida*
expensive *caro*
experience *la experiencia*
expiration date *la fecha de caducidad*
express service *el servicio rápido*
extension cord *el alargador*

extra *extra*
eye *el ojo*
eyebrow *la ceja*
eyelash *la pestaña*
eyeliner *el lápiz de ojos*

F

fabric *la tela*
face *la cara*
faint (verb) *desmayarse*
fairground *el parque de atracciones*
fall *el otoño*
family *la familia*
family room *la habitación familiar*
family ticket *la entrada familiar*
fan *el ventilador*
far *lejos*
fare *la tarifa*
farm *la granja*
farmer *el/la granjero/a*
fashion *la moda*
fast *rápido*
fast food *la comida rápida*
fat *la grasa*
father *el padre*
faucet *el grifo*
favorite *preferido*
February *febrero*
feel (verb) *sentir*
female *la mujer*
fence *la valla*
ferry *el ferry*
festivals *las fiestas*
fever *la fiebre*
field *el campo*
fill (verb) *llenar*
fillet *el filete*
film (roll of) *el carrete*
find (verb) *encontrar*
fine (legal) *la multa*

finger *el dedo*
finish (verb) *acabar; terminar*
fins *las aletas*
fire *el incendio*
fire alarm *la alarma de incendios*
fire department *los bomberos*
fire engine *el camión de bomberos*
fire escape *la salida de incendios*
fire extinguisher *el extintor*
firefighter *el/la bombero/a*
fire hydrant *la boca de riego*
first *primero*
first aid *los primeros auxilios*
first-aid box *el botiquín*
fish *los peces*
fishing *pescar*
fishing rod *la caña de pescar*
fish seller *la pescadería*
fitness *la forma física*
fitting room *el probador*
fix (verb) *arreglar*
flag *la bandera*
flash gun *el flash*
flashlight *la linterna*
flash photography *la fotografía con flash*
flat *bemol*
flat tire *el pinchazo*
flight *el vuelo*
flight attendant *la auxiliar de vuelo*
flight number *el número de vuelo*
flip-flops *las chanclas*
float *el flotador*
flood *la inundación*
floor *el suelo*
florist *el/la florista*
flowers *las flores*
flu *la gripe*
fly (verb) *volar*

fog *la niebla*
food *el alimento; la comida*
foot *el pie*
footpath *el sendero*
for *para*
foreign currency *las divisas*
forest *el bosque*
forget (verb) *olvidar*
fork *el tenedor*
form *la forma*
fortnight *quince días*
forward *el delantero centro*
fountain *la fuente*
fracture *la fractura*
fragile *frágil*
frame *la estructura*
free (no charge) *gratis*
free (not engaged) *libre*
freeze *la helada*
French press *la cafetera de émbolo*
fresh *fresco*
Friday *viernes*
fried *frito*
friend *el/la amigo/a*
friendly *amable*
from *de; desde*
front *delante, in front of delante de*
front door *la puerta principal*
frost *la escarcha*
frozen *congelado*
fruit *la fruta*
fry (verb) *freír*
frying pan *la sartén*
fuel gauge *el indicador del nivel de la gasolina*
full *lleno*
furniture store *la tienda de muebles*
fuse box *la caja de los plomos*

G

game *el juego*
garage *el garaje*
garbage can *el cubo de la basura*
garden *el jardín*
garlic *el ajo*
gas *el gas*
gasoline *la gasolina*
gas station *la gasolinera*
gate *la puerta*
gear shift *el cambio de marchas*
gift *el regalo*
gift store *la tienda de artículos de regalo*
gift-wrap *envuelto para regalo*
gin *la ginebra*
ginger *el jengibre*
giraffe *la jirafa*
girl *la chica*
girlfriend *la novia*
give (verb) *dar*
glass *el vaso*
glasses *las gafas*
gloss *brillante*
gloves *los guantes*
glue *la cola*
go (verb) *ir*
go clubbing *ir de discotecas*
goggles *las gafas de natación*
gold *el oro*
golf *el golf*
golf ball *la pelota de golf*
golf club *el palo de golf*
golf course *el campo de golf*
golf tee *el tee de golf*
good *bien; bueno*
goodbye *adiós*
good afternoon *buenas tardes*
good evening *buenas tardes*
good morning *buenos días*

goodnight *buenas noches*
GPS receiver *el navegador por satélite*
gram *el gramo*
grater *el rallador*
gray *gris*
graze *el rasguño*
Great Britain *Gran Bretaña*
green *verde*
greengrocery *la verdulería*
green slope *la pista para principiantes*
green tea *el té verde*
griddle pan *la plancha*
groceries *la compra*
ground *molido*
group *el grupo*
guarantee *la garantía*
guest *el/la invitado/a*
guide *el/la guía*
guidebook *la guía*
guided tour *el recorrido guiado*
gym *el gimnasio*

H

hail *el granizo*
hair *el pelo*
hairdresser's *la peluquería*
half *medio; la mitad*
hand *la mano*
handbag *el bolso*
handle *la manilla*
hand luggage *el equipaje de mano*
handsome *guapo*
happen (verb) *pasar*
happy *contento; feliz*
harbor *el puerto*
hard *duro*
hardware store *la ferretería*
hat *el sombrero*

hatchback el coche de cinco puertas
hate (verb) detestar
have (verb) tener
hayfever la alergia al polen
hazard lights las luces antiniebla
he él
head la cabeza
headache el dolor de cabeza
headlight el faro
headphones los auriculares
head rest el reposacabezas
health la salud
health insurance el seguro médico
hear (verb) oír
heart el corazón
heart condition la enfermedad cardíaca
heater la calefacción
heavy pesado
heel el talón
height la altura
hello hola
helmet el casco
help (verb) ayudar
herb la hierba
here aquí
high blood pressure la tensión alta
high chair la trona
high-speed train el tren de alta velocidad
highway la autopista
hiking el senderismo
hill la colina
hip la cadera
hockey el hockey
hold (verb) sujetar
home: at home en casa
hood la capucha
hood (car) el capó

horn el cláxon
horse el caballo
horseback riding montar a caballo
hospital el hospital
host el/la anfitrión/a
hot caliente
hot (spicy) picante
hot chocolate el cacao
hot drinks las bebidas calientes
hotel el hotel
hour la hora
house la casa
hovercraft el aerodeslizador
how? ¿cómo?
how many? ¿cuántos?
humid húmedo
hundred cien
hurricane el huracán
husband el marido
hydrofoil el aliscafo

I

I (1st person) yo
ice el hielo
ice cream el helado
ice-skating el patinaje sobre hielo
icy helado
ID el documento de identidad
ill enfermo
illness la enfermedad
immigration inmigración
in en
inbox la bandeja de entrada
inch la pulgada
induction session la sesión de introducción
infection la infección
in-flight meal la comida de avión
inhaler el inhalador
injection la inyección

injure (verb) *herir; lesionar*
injury *la lesión*
insect repellent *el repelente de insectos*
inside *dentro*
instructions *el modo de empleo*
insurance *el seguro*
insurance company *la compañía de seguros*
insurance policy *la póliza de seguros*
intensive care unit *la unidad de cuidados intensivos*
interest (verb) *interesar*
interesting *interesante*
internet café *el cibercafé*
interpreter *el/la intérprete*
into *dentro de*
inventory *el inventario*
iPod *el iPod*
iron *la plancha*
ironing board *la tabla de planchar*
island *la isla*
it *ello; lo/la*

J

jacket *la chaqueta*
jam *la mermelada*
January *enero*
jar *el tarro*
jaw *la mandíbula*
jazz club *el club de jazz*
jeans *los tejanos*
jellyfish *la medusa*
jet ski *la moto acuática*
jeweler *la joyería*
jewelry *las joyas*
jogging *el footing*
journey *el viaje*

juice *el zumo*
July *julio*
June *junio*

K

keep (verb) *mantener*
kettle *el hervidor de agua*
key *la llave*
keyboard *el teclado*
kidney *el riñón*
kilogram *el kilogramo*
kilometer *el kilómetro*
kitchen *la cocina*
knee *la rodilla*
knife *el cuchillo*
know (a fact) *saber*
know (people) *conocer*

L

labels *las etiquetas*
lake *el lago*
lamb *el cordero*
laptop *el portátil*
last *último*
last week *la semana pasada*
late *atrasado; tarde*
laugh (verb) *reír*
laundromat *a lavandería*
lawyer *el/la abogado/a*
leak *el escape*
learn (verb) *aprender*
leave *dejar*
left *la izquierda*
left luggage *la consigna*
leg *la pierna*
leisure *el ocio*
leisure activities *los pasatiempos*
lemon *el limón*
lemon grass *la citronela*
lemonade *la limonada*
length *la longitud*
lens *la lente*
letter carrier *el/la cartero/a*

lettuce *la lechuga*
library *la biblioteca*
lid *la tapa*
life jacket *el chaleco salvavidas*
lifeguard *el/la socorrista*
life ring *el salvavidas*
lift pass *el pase para
  el telesilla*
light *la luz*
light (not heavy) *ligero*
light (verb) *encender*
light bulb *la bombilla*
lighter *el mechero*
lighthouse *el faro*
lights switch *el commutador de
  luces*
like (verb) *gustar*
lime *el tilo*
liquid *el detergente líquido*
list *la lista*
listen (verb) *escuchar*
liter *el litro*
little *poco*
living room *el cuarto de estar*
load (verb) *cargar*
loan *el préstamo*
lock *la cerradura*
lockers *las taquillas*
log on (verb) *iniciar sesión*
log out (verb) *cerrar sesión*
long *largo*
look for (verb) *buscar*
lose (verb) *perder*
lost property *los objetos
  perdidos*
lounge chair *la tumbona*
love (verb) *amar*
low *bajo*
luggage *el equipaje*
luggage rack *el portaequipajes*
lunch *la comida*
lunch menu *el menú
  de la comida*

M

magazine *la revista*
mail *el correo*
mailbox *el buzón*
main course *el plato principal*
make (verb) *hacer*
makeup *el maquillaje*
male *el hombre*
mallet *el mazo*
man *el hombre*
manager *el/la jefe/a*
mango *el mango*
manicure *la manicura*
manual *manual*
manuscript *el manuscrito*
many *muchos*
map *el mapa*
March *marzo*
marina *el puerto deportivo*
market *el mercado*
marmalade *la mermelada*
married *casado*
mascara *el rímel*
massage *el masaje*
match (light) *la cerilla*
match (sport) *el partido*
mattress *el colchon*
May *mayo*
maybe *quizá*
mayonnaise *la mayonesa*
meal *la comida*
measure *la medida*
meat *la carne*
meatballs *las albóndigas*
mechanic *el/la mecánico/a*
medicine *la medicina*
memory card *la tarjeta
  de memoria*
memory stick *la llave USB*
menu *el menú*
message *el mensaje*
metal *el metal*
metre *el metro*

microwave *el microondas*
middle *el centro*
midnight *la medianoche*
migraine *la jaqueca*
mile *la milla*
milk *la leche*
mineral water *el agua mineral*
mini bar *el minibar*
mint *la menta*
minute *el minuto*
mirror *el espejo*
mistake *el error*
misty *niebla*
mixing bowl *el bol*
mole (medical) *el lunar*
Monday *el lunes*
money *el dinero*
monkey *el mono*
month *el mes*
monument *el monumento*
mooring *el atracadero*
mop *la fregona*
more *más*
morning *la mañana*
mosquito *el mosquito*
mosquito net *la mosquitera*
mother *la madre*
motorcycle *la moto*
mountain *la montaña*
mountain bike *la bicicleta de montaña*
mouse *el ratón*
mouth *la boca*
mouthwash *el enjuague bucal*
move *el turno*
movie *la película*
movie theater *el cine*
much *mucho*
mug *la taza*
murder *el delito*
muscles *los músculos*
museum *el museo*
mushroom *la seta*

music *la música*
musician *el músico*
mustard *la mostaza*
my *mi*
myself *yo mismo*

N

nail *la uña*
nail clippers *los cortaúñas*
nail scissors *las tijeras para las uñas*
name *el nombre*
napkin *la servilleta*
narrow *estrecho*
national park *el parque nacional*
natural *el becuadro*
nausea *la naúsea*
navigate (verb) *navegar*
near *cerca*
nearby *por aquí cerca*
neck *el cuello*
necklace *el collar*
need (verb) *necesitar*
nervous *nerviosa*
net *la red*
network *la red*
never *nunca*
new *nuevo*
news *la noticia*
newsagent *la tienda de prensa*
newspaper *el periódico*
next *próximo*
next to *cerca de*
next week *la semana que viene*
nice (person) *simpático*
night *la noche*
nightclub *el club nocturno*
no *no*
no entry *prohibida la entrada*

noisy *ruidoso*
noon *el mediodía*
normal *normal*
north *el norte*
nose *la nariz*
nosebleed *la hemorragia nasal*
not *no*
notebook *el cuaderno*
nothing *nada*
November *noviembre*
now *ahora*
number *el número*
nurse *el/la enfermero/a*
nuts *los frutos secos*

O

oar *el remo*
oats *la avena*
occupation *la profesión*
occupied *ocupado*
ocean *el océano*
October *octubre*
octopus *el pulpo*
of *de*
office *la oficina*
often *con frecuencia*
oil *el aceite*
ointment *la pomada*
ok *vale*
old *viejo*
olive oil *el aceite de oliva*
olives *las aceitunas*
omelet *la tortilla*
on *en*
one *uno;* this one/that one
   éste/ése
one-way ticket
   el billete de ida
onion *la cebolla*
only *sólo*
onto *sobre*
open (verb) *abrir*
opening hours *el horario*

opening times *horario*
   de apertura
opera *la ópera*
opera house *el teatro de*
   la ópera
operation *la operación*
opposite *enfrente de*
or *o*
orange *la naranja*
orange juice *el zumo*
   de naranja
order (verb) *pedir*
our *nuestro*
out *fuera*
outside *fuera*
oven *el horno*
oven mitts *las manoplas para*
   el horno
over *por*
over there *por allí*
overdraft *el descubierto*
overhead bin *el compartimento*
   portaequipajes
overtake (verb) *adelantar*
owe (verb) *deber*

P

package *el paquete*
pack of cards *la baraja*
pads *las rodilleras*
pail *el dolor*
painkiller *el calmante*
painting *la pintura*
pair *el par*
pajamas *el pijama*
pan *la bandeja*
pan fried *frito con*
   poco aceite
pants *los pantalones*
panty hose *el panti*
paper *el papel*
papers (identity)
   la documentación; los papeles

parents *los padres*
park (noun) *el parque*
park (verb) *aparcar*
parka *el chaquetón*
parking lot *el aparcamiento*
parking meter
  el parquímetro
parmesan *el parmesano*
parsley *el perejil*
partner *el/la compañero/a*
pass *el pase*
passenger *el/la pasajero/a*
passport *el pasaporte*
passport control *el control de
  pasaportes*
pasta *la pasta*
pastry *el pastel*
path *el camino*
patient *el/la paciente*
pause *la pausa*
pay (verb) *pagar*
payment *el pago*
payphone *el teléfono
  público*
peanut *el cacahuete*
peanut butter *la mantequilla
  de cacahuetes*
pear *la pera*
pedestrian crossing *el paso
  de peatones*
pedicure *la pedicura*
peel (verb) *pelar*
peeler *el pelador*
pen *el bolígrafo*
pencil *el lápiz*
people *las personas*
pepper *la pimienta*
perfume *el perfume*
perhaps *quizás*
pet *el animal doméstico*
pharmacist *el/la farmacéutico/a*
pharmacy *la farmacia*
phone card *la tarjeta telefónica*

photo album *el álbum
  de fotos*
photo frame *el marco*
photograph *la fotografía*
photography *la fotografía*
pianist *el/la pianista*
picnic *el picnic*
picnic basket *la canasta
  de la comida*
pie *el pastel*
piece *el trozo de*
pill *la pastilla*
pillow *la almohada*
pilot *el/la piloto*
PIN *el pin*
pint *la pinta*
pitch *el campo de críquet*
pitch a tent (verb) *montar
  una tienda*
pitcher *la jarra*
pizza *la pizza*
place *el lugar*
plane *el cepillo*
planet *el planeta*
plants *las plantas*
plate *el plato*
platform *el andén*
play *la obra de teatro*
play (theater) *representar*
play (verb) *jugar*
pleasant *agradable*
please *por favor*
plug (electric) *el enchufe*
plum *la ciruela*
plumber *el/la fontanero/a*
pocket *el bolsillo*
point *el punto*
police *la policía*
police car *el coche patrulla*
police officer *el policía/la policía*
police station *la comisaría*
policy *la póliza*
pool: swimming pool *la piscina*

popcorn *las palomitas de maíz*
pork *el cerdo*
porridge *las gachas de avena*
porter *el botones*
portion *la ración*
possible *posible*
post office *la oficina de correos*
postage *el franqueo*
postcard *la postal*
potato *la patata*
potato chips *las patata fritas*
poultry *las aves*
pound *la libra*
pour (verb) *echar*
powder *el detergente en polvo*
power *la corriente eléctrica*
power outage *el corte de luz*
prefer (verb) *preferir*
pregnancy test *la prueba del embarazo*
pregnant *embarazada*
prescription *la receta*
present *el regalo*
press *la prensa*
pretty *bonito*
price *el precio*
price list *la lista de precios*
print *la copia*
print (verb) *imprimir*
proud *orgulloso*
prove (verb) *levar*
province *la provincia*
pump (bicycle) *la mancha*
public holiday *el día festivo*
purple *morado*
push *empuje*
put (verb) *poner*

Q

quarter *el cuarto*
quick *rápido*
quite *bastante*

R

rabbit *el conejo*
race *la carrera*
racecourse *el hipódromo*
rack *el soporte*
radiator *el radiador*
radio *la radio*
rail *el raíl*
railroad *el ferrocarril*
rain boots *las botas de agua*
rain forest *la selva tropical*
raining *lloviendo*
rape *la violación*
rarely *rara vez*
rash *el sarpullido*
raspberry *la frambuesa*
rat *la rata*
raw *crudo*
razor *la maquinilla de afeitar*
read (verb) *leer*
ready *listo*
real estate office *la agencia inmobiliaria*
reboot (verb) *reiniciar*
receipt *el recibo*
receive (verb) *recibir*
reception *la recepción*
receptionist *el/la recepcionista*
recommend *recomendar*
record *el récord*
record store *la tienda de discos*
recycling bin *el cubo para reciclar*
red *rojo*
reduction *el descuento*
refrigerator *el frigorífico*
region *la región*

registration number (car) *la matrícula*
relatives *los parientes*
release (verb) *soltar*
remote control *el mando a distancia*
rent (verb) *alquilar*
repair (noun) *la reparación*
repair (verb) *arreglar*
report (noun) *la denuncia*
report (verb) *informar de*
research *la investigación*
reservation *la reserva*
rest *la pausa*
restaurant *el restaurante*
toilet *los aseos*
resuscitation *la boca a boca*
retired *jubilado*
return *el resto*
return ticket *el billete de ida y vuelta*
reverse (verb) *dar marcha atrás*
rewind *el botón para rebobinar*
rib *la costilla*
rice *el arroz*
rides *las atracciones*
right (correct) *correcto*
right (direction) *la derecha*
ring *el anillo*
rinse (verb) *aclarar*
ripe *maduro*
river *el río*
road *la carretera*
road signs *las señales de tráfico*
roadwork *las obras*
roast *el asado*
rob (verb) *asaltar*
robbery *el asalto*
robe *la toga*
rock *la roca*
rock climbing *la escalada*
roll (of film) *el carrete*

romance *la película romántica*
roof *el techo*
roofrack *la baca*
room *la habitación*
room key *la llave de la habitación*
root *la raíz*
rope *la cuerda*
round *redondo*
router *el enrutador; el rúter*
row *la fila*
rowing machine *la máquina de remo*
ruby *el rubí*
rug *la alfombra*
run *la carrera*
rush *el junco*

S

sad *triste*
safe *seguro*
sailboat *el barco de vela*
sailing *navegar*
salad *la ensalada*
salami *el salami*
salesperson *el/la dependiente/a*
salmon *el salmón*
salt *la sal*
salted *salado*
same *mismo*
sand *la arena*
sandal *la sandalia*
sandwich *el bocadillo*
sanitary napkin *la compresa*
satellite navigation *la navegación por satélite*
satellite TV *la televisión por satélite*
Saturday *el sábado*
sauce *la salsa*
saucepan *la cacerola*
saucer *el plato*
sauna *la sauna*

sausage *la salchicha*
sauté (verb) *saltear*
save (verb) (soccer) *parar*
savings account *la cuenta de ahorros*
savory *salado*
say (verb) *decir*
scale *la báscula*
scan *el escáner*
scared *asustado*
scarf *la bufanda*
school *el colegio*
scissors *las tijeras*
scoop *la bola*
scooter *la vespa*
score *la partitura*
scuba diving *el buceo*
sea *el mar*
seafood *el marisco*
search (verb) *buscar*
season *la estación*
seat *el asiento*
second (position) *segundo*
second (time) *el segundo*
second floor *la primera planta*
security *la seguridad*
sedan *el turismo*
see (verb) *ver*
seedless *sin pepitas*
seed *la semilla*
sell (verb) *vender*
sell-by date *la fecha de caducidad*
send (verb) *enviar*
send off *la expulsión*
senior citizen *el/la pensionista*
sensitive *sensible*
sentence *la sentencia*
separately *por separado*
September *septiembre*
serious *grave*
serve *el servicio*
server *el camarero/ la camarera*

services *los servicios*
set *el decorado*
sew (verb) *coser*
shampoo *el champú*
shark *el tiburón*
sharp *sostenido*
shaving foam *la espuma de afeitar*
she *ella*
sheet *la sábana bajera*
shelf *el estante*
shelves *los estantes*
sherbet *el sorbete*
shirt *la camisa*
shoe *el zapato*
shoe store *la zapatería*
shopping *ir de compras*
shopping center *el centro comercial*
short *corto*
shorts *los pantalones cortos*
shoulder *el hombro*
shout (verb) *gritar*
shower *la ducha*
shower gel *el gel de ducha*
shy *tímido*
sick *enfermo*
side *el lado*
side-by-side refrigerator *el frigorífico congelador*
side effect *el efecto secundario*
side dish *la guarnición*
sidewalk *la acera*
sightseeing *el turismo*
sign *el letrero*
signal *la señal*
signature *la firma*
signpost *señalizar*
silk *la seda*
silver *la plata*
singer *el/la cantante*
single bed *la cama individual*

single room *la habitación individual*
sink *el lavabo*
siren *la sirena*
sister *la hermana*
size (clothes) *la talla*
size (shoes) *el número*
skate *el patín*
sketch *el boceto*
ski *el esquí*
ski (verb) *esquiar*
ski boots *las botas de esquí*
ski slope *la pista de esquí*
skin *la piel*
skirt *la falda*
skis *los esquíes*
sleeper berth *la litera*
sleeping *dormir*
sleeping bag *el saco de dormir*
sleeping pill *el somnífero*
slice *la loncha; el trozo*
slide *el tobogán*
slip *la combinación*
slippers *las pantuflas*
slope *la ladera*
slow *lento*
slow down *disminuir la velocidad*
small *pequeño*
smartphone *el teléfono inteligente*
smile *la sonrisa*
smoke *el humo*
smoke (verb) *fumar*
smoke alarm *la alarma de incendios*
smoking area *zona de fumadores*
snack *el tentempié*
snack bar *la barrita*
snake *la serpiente*
sneakers *las bambas*
sneeze *el estornudo*
snore (verb) *roncar*

snorkel *el tubo de buceo*
snow *la nieve*
snow (verb) *nevar*
snowboard *la tabla de snowboard*
so *tan*
soak (verb) *poner a remojo*
soap *el jabón*
soccer *el fútbol*
socks *los calcetines*
soda water *la soda*
sofa *el sofá*
sofa bed *el sofá-cama*
soft *blando*
soft drinks *los refrescos*
soil *la tierra*
some *unos*
somebody; someone *alguien*
something *algo*
sometimes *a veces*
son *el hijo*
song *la canción*
soon *pronto*
sorry: I'm sorry *lo siento*
soup *la sopa*
sour *amargo*
south *el sur*
souvenir *el recuerdo*
Spain *España*
Spanish *español*
spare tire *la rueda de repuesto*
spatula *la espátula*
speak (verb) *hablar*
speaker *el/la orador/a*
specials *los platos del día*
speed limit *la velocidad máxima*
speedometer *el velocímetro*
spices *las especias*
spider *la araña*
spinach *la espinaca*
spine *la espina dorsal*
splint *la tablilla*
splinter *la astilla*
spoke *el radio*

sponge *la esponja*
spoon *la cuchara*
sport *el deporte*
sports center *el centro deportivo*
sprain *el esguince*
spring *la primavera*
square *el cuadrado*
square (in town) *la plaza*
staff *el personal*
stage *el escenario*
staircase *la escalera*
stairs *las escaleras*
stalls *el patio de butacas*
stamp *el sello*
stand *el soporte*
start (verb) *empezar*
statement *la declaración*
station (railway) *la estación*
station (underground) *la boca de metro*
statue *la estatua*
stay (verb) *quedarse*
steak *la rodaja*
steamed *al vapor*
steering wheel *el volante*
sterling *la libra*
stew *el guiso*
sting *el aquijón*
stir (verb) *remover*
stir-fry *la fritura*
stolen *robado*
stomach *el estómago*
stomach ache *el dolor de estómago*
stone *la piedra*
stop! *¡alto!*
stop (verb) *parar*
store *la tienda*
stormy *tormenta*
straight *recto*
strap *el tirante*
strawberry *la fresa*
street *la calle*

street map *el plano*
street sign *la señal de tráfico*
stress *el estrés*
string *el cordel*
strong *fuerte*
student *el/la estudiante*
student card *el carné de estudiante*
study *el despacho*
stuffed animal *el peluche*
suburb *la periferia*
subway *el metro*
subway map *el plano del metro*
suit *el traje*
suitcase *la maleta*
summer *el verano*
sun *el sol*
sunbathe (verb) *tomar el sol*
sunbed *la cama de rayos ultravioletas*
sunblock *la crema protectora total*
sunburn *la quemadura del sol*
Sunday *el domingo*
sunflower oil *el aceite de girasol*
sunglasses *las gafas de sol*
sunhat *el sombrero*
sunrise *el amanecer*
sunscreen *la crema con filtro solar*
sunset *la puesta de sol*
sunshine *el sol*
supermarket *el supermercado*
support *el soporte*
suppositories *los supositorios*
surf *la rompiente*
surf (verb) *hacer surf*
surfboard *la tabla de surf*
surgeon *el/la cirujano/a*
surgery *la consulta*
surprised *sorprendido*

sweater *el jersey*
sweatshirt *la sudadera*
sweep (verb) *barrer*
sweet *dulce*
sweet potato *el boniato*
swim (verb) *nadar*
swimsuit *el bañador*
swings *los columpios*
switch *el interruptor*

T

table *la mesa*
tablet *la pastilla*
tailor *el/la sastre/a*
take (verb) *tomar*
take off (verb) *despegar;*
  quitarse (clothes)
talk (verb) *conversar; hablar*
tall *alto*
tampon *el tampón*
tan *el bronceado*
tank *el tanque*
taste (verb) *probar*
tax *el impuesto*
taxi *el taxi*
taxi driver *el/la taxista*
taxi stand *la parada*
  de taxis
tea *el té*
teabag *la bolsita de té*
team *el equipo*
teapot *la tetera*
teaspoon *la cucharilla*
  de café
teeth *los dientes*
telephone *el teléfono*
telephone box *la cabina*
television *la televisión*
television set *el televisor*
tell (verb) *decir*
temperature *la temperatura*
tennis *el tenis*
tennis ball *la pelota de tenis*

tennis court *la pista*
  de tenis
tennis racket *la raqueta*
  de tenis
tent *la tienda*
terminal *la terminal*
test *el análisis*
text (SMS) *el mensaje*
  de texto (SMS)
than *que*
thank (verb) *agradecer*
thanks *las gracias*
thank you *gracias*
that *ese/a*
their *su/sus*
them *ellos/as*
there *allí*
thermometer
  el termómetro
they *ellos/as*
thick *grueso*
thief *el ladrón*
thin *delgado*
thing *la cosa*
third floor *la segunda*
  planta
this *éste/a*
throat *la garganta*
throat lozenge *la pastilla para*
  la garganta
through *por*
throw *el derribo*
thumb *el pulgar*
Thursday *el jueves*
ticket *el billete*
ticket gates *la barrera*
ticket inspector *el revisor*
ticket office *la taquilla*
tide *la marea*
tie *la corbata*
tight *ajustado*
tile *la ficha*
time *el tiempo; la hora*

timetable *el horario*
tin (can) *la lata*
tip *la punta*
tissue *el pañuelo de papel*
to *a*
to sign (verb) *firmar*
toast *el pan tostado*
toaster *el tostador*
tobacco *el tabaco*
tobacconist *el estanco*
today *hoy*
toe *el dedo del pie*
toilet *el aseo*
toilet paper *el rollo de papel higiénico*
toiletries *los artículos de tocador*
toll *peaje (m)*
tomato *el tomate*
tomato sauce *el ketchup*
tomorrow *mañana*
tongue *la lengua*
tonight *esta noche*
too *demasiado*
too (also) *también*
tooth *el diente*
toothache *el dolor de muelas*
toothbrush *el cepillo de dientes*
toothpaste *el dentífrico*
tour *el recorrido; el viaje*
tour bus *el autobús turístico*
tour guide *el/la guía turístico/a*
tourist *el turista*
tourist attraction *la atracción turística*
tourist information office *oficina de turismo*
towards *hacia*
towels *las toallas*
town *la ciudad*

town center *el centro*
town hall *el ayuntamiento*
toy *el juguete*
track *la vía*
traffic *el tráfico*
traffic circle *la glorieta*
traffic jam *el atasco*
traffic lights *el semáforo*
train *el tren*
train station *la estación de tren*
tram *el tranvía*
transportation *el transporte*
trash *la papelera*
travel (verb) *viajar*
travel agent *el/la agente de viajes*
travel-sickness pills *las píldoras para el mareo*
tray *la bandeja*
tree *el árbol*
trekking *el paseo*
tripod *el trípode*
trout *la trucha*
trunk (car) *el maletero*
try *el ensayo*
try (verb) *intentar*
T-shirt *la camiseta*
tub *la tarrina*
tube *el tubo*
Tuesday *el martes*
tumble dryer *la secadora*
tuna *el atún*
turn (verb) *tornear*
tweezers *las pinzas*
twin beds *dos camas*
twin room *la habitación con dos camas individuales*
tire *el neumático*
tire pressure *la presión de los neumáticos*

U

ugly *feo*
umbrella *el paraguas*
uncle *el tío*
under *debajo de*
underpass *el paso subterráneo*
undershirt *la camiseta de tirantes*
understand *comprender*
underwear *la ropa interior*
uniform *el uniforme*
United States *Estados Unidos*
university *la universidad*
unleaded *sin plomo*
until *hasta*
up (not down) *arriba*
upset *triste*
urgent *urgente*
us *nosotros*
use (verb) *usar*
useful *útil*
usual *habitual*
usually *habitualmente*

V

vacancy *la habitación libre*
vacation *las vacaciones;* **on vacation** *de vacaciones*
vacuum flask *el termo*
valid *válido*
valuables *los objetos de valor*
value *el valor*
vegetables *la verdura*
vegetarian *vegetariano*
veggie burger *la hamburguesa vegetariana*
vehicle *el vehículo*
venetian blind *la persiana de lamas*

very *muy; mucho*
vet *el/la veterinario/a*
video game *el videojuego*
view *la vista*
village *el pueblo*
vinegar *el vinagre*
vineyard *la viña*
virus *el virus*
visa *la visa*
vision *la vista*
visit *la visita*
visitor *el/la visitante*
vitamins *las vitaminas*
voice message *el mensaje de voz*
volume *el volumen*
vomit (verb) *vomitar*

W

wait (verb) *esperar*
waiting room *la sala de espera*
wake up (verb) *despertarse*
walk *el paso*
walk (verb) *andar*
wall *la barrera*
ward *la sala*
warm *caliente; caluroso*
wash (verb) *fregar*
washing machine *la lavadora*
wasp *la avispa*
watch *el reloj*
watch (verb) *mirar*
water *el agua*
water bottle *la cantimplora*
waterfall *la cascada*
watermelon *la sandía*
waterskiing *el esquí acuático*

watersports
  los deportes acuáticos
water valve
  la llave de paso
water wings
  el manguito
wave *la ola*
wax *la cera*
we *nosotros*
weak *débil*
weather
  el tiempo
website
  la página web
wedding *la boda*
week *la semana*
weigh (verb) *pesar*
weight *la pesa*
well *bien*
west *el oeste*
wet *húmedo*
wetsuit *el traje
  de buzo*
wet wipe *la toallita
  húmeda*
whale *la ballena*
what? *¿qué?*
wheat *el trigo*
wheel *la rueda*
wheelchair *la silla
  de ruedas*
wheelchair access *el acceso
  para sillas de ruedas*
wheelchair ramp *la rampa para
  sillas de ruedas*
when? *¿cuándo?*
where? *¿dónde?*
which? *¿qué?; ¿cuál?*
whisk *el batidor*
whiskey *el whisky*
white *blanco*
who? *¿quién?*
whole *entero*

whole-wheat bread *el
  pan moreno*
why? *¿por qué?*
wide *ancho*
widescreen TV *el televisor
  de pantalla ancha*
width
  la anchura
wife *la esposa*
win (verb) *ganar*
wind *el viento*
window *la ventana*
window seat *el asiento
  de ventanilla*
windshield
  el parabrisas
windshield wiper
  el limpiaparabrisas
windsurfing
  hacer windsurf
wine *el vino*
wine glass *la copa
  de vino*
wine list *la lista
  de vinos*
winter *el invierno*
winter sports *los deportes
  de invierno*
wipe (verb) *pasar
  la bayeta*
with *con*
withdraw (verb) *retirar*
without *sin*
witness *el testigo*
woman *la mujer*
wood *el bosque*
wool *la lana*
work *el trabajo*
work (verb) *trabajar*
worried *preocupado*
worse *peor*
wrap (gift) *envolver*
wrist *la muñeca*

wrist watch *el reloj de muñeca*
write (verb) *escribir*
wrong (not right) *incorrecto*

X, Y, Z

X-ray *la radiografía*
yacht *el yate*
year *el año*
yellow *amarillo*
yes *sí*

yesterday *ayer*
yogurt *el yogur*
you *tú; vosotros*
young *joven*
your *tu; vuestro*
zebra crossing *el paso de zebra*
zero *cero*
zipper *la cremallera*
zone *la zona*
zoo *el zoológico*
zucchini *el calabacín*

The gender of a Spanish noun is indicated by the word for the: el (masculine) and la (feminine) or los (masculine plural) and las (feminine plural). Spanish adjectives vary according to the gender and number of the word they describe. Most ending in "o" adopt an "a" ending in the feminine form; those ending in "e" usually stay the same.

A

a *to*
abajo *below*
abeja (f) *bee*
abogado/a (m/f) *lawyer*
abonar *to pay*
abrebotellas (m)
  bottle opener
abrelatas (m)
  can opener
abrigo (m) *coat*
abril (m) *April*
abrir *to open*
aburrido *bored*
acabar *to finish*
acampar *to camp*
acantilado (m) *cliff*
accesso (m) *access*
accidente (m) *accident*
accidente de coche (m) *car crash*
aceite (m) *oil*
aceite de girasol (m) *sunflower oil*
aceite de oliva (m) *olive oil*
aceitunas (f pl) *olives*
acera (f) *sidewalk*
aclarar *to rinse*
actividades (f pl) *activities*
actor (m) *actor*
actriz (f) *actress*
adaptador (m) *adapter*
adelantar *to overtake*
adiós *goodbye*

aduana (f) *customs*
adulto *adult*
aeróbic (m)
  aerobics
aerodeslizador (m)
  hovercraft
aeropuerto (m) *airport*
afeitarse *to shave*
agencia inmobiliaria (f)
  real estate office
agenda (f) *day planner*
agente de policía (m/f)
  police officer
agente de viajes (m/f)
  travel agent
agosto (m) *August*
agradable *pleasant*
agradecer *to thank*
agua (f) *water*
agua embotellada (f)
  bottled water
agua mineral (f)
  mineral water
aguacate (m) *avocado*
ahogarse *to choke*
ahora *now*
airbag (m) *airbag*
aire acondicionado (m)
  air conditioning
ajo (m) *garlic*
ajustado *tight*
al otro lado *across*

alargador (m)
  extension cord
alarma (f) *alarm*
alarma de incendios (f)
  smoke alarm
albahaca (f) *basil*
albañil (m/f) *construction worker*
albaricoque (m) *apricot*
albóndigas (f pl) *meatballs*
albornoz (m) *bath robe*
álbum de fotos (m)
  photo album
alergia (f) *allergy*
alergia al polen (f) *hayfever*
alérgico *allergic*
aletas (f pl) *fins*
alfombra (f) *rug*
algo *anything; something*
algodón (m) *cotton*
alguien *somebody; someone*
alimento (m) *food*
aliño (m) *dressing*
aliscafo (m) *hydrofoil*
allí *there*
almeja (f) *clam*
almohada (f) *pillow*
almuerzo (m) *lunch*
alojamiento (m) *accommodation*
alquilar *to rent*
alquiler de coches (m)
  car rental
alrededor de *about; around*
altitud (f) *altitude*
¡alto! *stop!*
alto *tall*
altura (f) *height*
amable *friendly*
amanecer (m) *sunrise*
amar *to love; to like*
amargo *bitter; sour*
ambulancia (f) *ambulance*
amigo/a (m/f) *friend*
ampolla (f) *blister*

análisis (m) *test*
análisis de sangre (m)
  blood test
ancho *wide*
anchura (f) *width*
andar *to walk*
andén (m) *platform*
anfitrión/a (m/f) *host*
anillo (m) *ring*
animal doméstico (m) *pet*
animales (m pl) *animals*
año (m) *year*
antes de *before*
antibióticos (m pl)
  antibiotics
anticoncepción (f)
  contraception
antiguo *old; ancient*
apagar *to turn off*
aparcamiento (m)
  parking lot; parking
aparcamiento para bicicletas
  (m) *bike rack*
aparcamiento para minusválidos
  (m) *disabled parking*
aparcar *to park*
apartamento (m) *apartment*
aperitivos (m pl) *bar snacks*
aplaudir *to applaud*
aplicación (f) *application*
apoyabrazos (m) *arm rest*
aprender *to learn*
aquí *here*
aquijón (m) *sting*
araña (f) *spider*
arándano (m) *blueberry*
árbol (m) *tree*
arco (m) *arch; arc*
área (f) *area*
arena (f) *sand*
armario (m) *closet*
arquitecto/a (m/f) *architect*
arquitectura (f) *architecture*

arrecife de coral (m) *coral reef*
arreglar *to fix; to mend; to repair*
arreglos (m pl) *arrangements*
arroz (m) *rice*
arroz integral (m) *brown rice*
arte (m) *art*
**artículos de tocador
(m pl)** *toiletries*
**artículos deportivos
(m pl)** *sports*
artritis (f) *arthritis*
asado (m) *roast*
asaltar *to rob*
asalto (m) *robbery*
asar a la parrilla *to broil*
ascensor (m) *elevator*
aseos (m) *restrooms*
asiento (m) *seat*
asiento de pasillo (m) *aisle seat*
asistir *to attend*
asma (f) *asthma*
aspecto (m) *appearance*
astilla (f) *splinter*
asustado *scared*
ataque (m) *attack*
atleta (m/f) *athlete*
atracadero (m) *mooring*
atracción turística (f)
tourist attraction
atracciones (f pl) *rides*
atrasado *late*
atún (m) *tuna*
auriculares (m pl) *headphones*
Australia *Australia*
autobús (m) *bus*
autobús turístico (m) *tour bus*
autocar (m) *coach*
automático *automatic*
autopista (f) *highway*
auxiliar de vuelo (m/f)
flight attendant
avena (f) *oats*
avenida (f) *avenue*

avergonzado *embarrassed*
avería (f) *breakdown*
aves (f pl) *poultry*
avión (m) *airplane*
avispa (f) *wasp*
ayer *yesterday*
ayuda *help*
ayudante (m/f) *assistant*
ayudar *to help*
azul *blue*

B

baca (f) *roofrack*
bacalao (m) *cod*
bádminton (m) *badminton*
baguette (f) *baguette*
bailar *to dance*
bajar *to download*
bajo *low*
balcón (m) *balcony*
ballena (f) *whale*
ballet (m) *ballet*
balón (m) *ball*
baloncesto (m) *basketball*
bañador (m) *swimsuit*
banco (m) *bank; bench*
bandeja (f) *tray*
bandeja de entrada (f) *inbox*
bandeja de horno (f)
cookie sheet
bandera (f) *flag*
bañera (f) *bathtub*
baño (m) *bath; bathroom*
bar (m) *bar; pub*
baraja (f) *pack of cards*
barato *cheap*
barbacoa (f) *barbecue*
barbero/a (m/f) *barber*
barbilla (f) *chin*
barca (f) *small boat*
barca de remos (f)
rowing boat
barco (m) *boat; ship*

barco de recreo (m) *pleasure boat*
barco de vela (m) *sailing boat*
barrer *to sweep*
barrera (f) *ticket gates; wall*
barrita (f) *snack bar*
báscula (f) *scale*
bastante *enough; quite*
bastones (m pl) *poles (ski)*
baya (f) *berry*
bebé (m/f) *baby*
beber *to drink*
bebidas (f pl) *drinks*
bebidas alcohólicas (f pl) *alcoholic drinks*
bebidas calientes (f pl) *hot drinks*
becuadro (m) *natural (music)*
béisbol (m) *baseball*
bemol (m) *flat (music)*
berenjena (f) *eggplant*
biblioteca (f) *library*
bicicleta (f) *bicycle*
bicicleta de montaña (f) *mountain bike*
bicicleta elíptica (f) *cross trainer*
bicicleta estática (f) *exercise bike*
bidé (m) *bidet*
bien *alright; good*
bikini (m) *bikini*
billete de autobús (m) *bus ticket*
billete de ida (m) *one-way ticket*
billete de ida y vuelta (m) *return ticket*
blanco *white*
blando *soft*
blusa (f) *blouse*
boca (f) *mouth*

boca a boca (f) *resuscitation*
boca de metro (f) *station (subway)*
boca de riego (f) *fire hydrant*
bocadillo (m) *sandwich*
bocado (m) *bit*
boceto (m) *sketch*
boda (f) *wedding*
bol (m) *mixing bowl*
bola (f) *scoop*
bolígrafo (m) *pen*
bollo (m) *bun*
bolos (m pl) *bowling*
bolsa (f) *bag*
bolsa de viaje (f) *duffel bag*
bolsillo (m) *pocket*
bolsita de té (f) *teabag*
bolso (m) *handbag*
bombero/a (m/f) *firefighter*
bomberos (m pl) *fire department*
bombilla (f) *light bulb*
bombón (m) *chocolate*
boniato (m) *sweet potato*
bonito *attractive; pretty*
bordo: a bordo *on board*
bosque (m) *forest; wood*
bota (f) *boot (footwear)*
botas de agua (f pl) *rain boots*
botas de esquí (f pl) *ski boots*
bote (m) *dinghy*
botella (f) *bottle*
botiquín (m) *first-aid box*
botón (m) *button*
botones (m/f) *porter*
boutique (f) *boutique*
boya (f) *buoy*
brazo (m) *arm*
brécol (m) *broccoli*
brillante *bright; glossy*
brioche (m) *brioche*
británico *British*
broche (m) *brooch*

bronceado (m) *tan*
bronceador (m) *suntan lotion*
brújula (f) *compass*
buceo (m) *scuba diving*
buenas noches *good night*
buenas tardes *good evening*
bueno *good; tasty*
buenos días *good morning*
bufanda (f) *scarf*
buffet (m) *buffet*
buffet de desayuno (m) *breakfast buffet*
bulbo (m) *bulb*
buscar *to look for*
busto (m) *bust*
buzón (m) *mailbox*

C

caballo (m) *horse*
cabeza (f) *head*
cabina (f) *cabin; telephone box*
cable (m) *cable*
cacahuete (m) *peanut*
cacao (m) *cocoa*
cacerola (f) *saucepan*
cada *each; every*
cadera (f) *hip*
café (m) *coffee*
café solo (m) *black coffee*
cafetería (f) *café; snack bar*
caja (f) *box; checkout (supermarket)*
caja de los plomos (f) *fuse box*
cajero/a (m/f) *checker*
cajero automático (m) *cash machine*
cajón (m) *drawer*
calabacín (m) *zucchini*
calabaza butternut (f) *butternut squash*

calambre (m) *cramp*
calcetines (m pl) *socks*
calculadora (f) *calculator*
calefacción (f) *heater*
calefacción central (f) *central heating*
calendario (m) *calendar*
caliente *hot*
calle (f) *street*
calmado *calm*
calmante (m) *painkiller*
caluroso *warm; hot (weather)*
calzoncillos (m pl) *briefs*
cama (f) *bed*
cama de matrimonio (f) *double bed*
cama de rayos ultravioletas (f) *sunbed*
cama individual (f) *single bed*
cámara (f) *camera*
cámara de usar y tirar (f) *disposable camera*
cámara digital (f) *digital camera*
camarero/a (m/f) *server*
camarote (m) *cabin (boat)*
cambiar *to change; to replace*
cambio (m) *change; exchange rate*
cambio de marchas (m) *gear shift*
camino (m) *path*
camión de bomberos (m) *fire engine*
camisa (f) *shirt*
camiseta de tirantes (f) *undershirt*
camisola (f) *camisole*
camping (m) *campsite*
camping para caravanas (m) *camper van site*
campo (m) *field*
campo de críquet (m) *cricket pitch*
campo de golf (m) *golf course*

Canadá *Canada*
caña de pescar (f) *fishing rod*
canal (m) *channel (TV)*
canasta (f) *basket*
canasta de la comida (f)
  picnic basket
canción (f) *song*
canela (f) *cinnamon*
cangrejo (m) *crab*
canoa (f) *canoe*
cantante (m/f) *singer*
cantidad (f) *amount*
cantimplora (f) *water bottle*
capital (f) *capital city*
capó (m) *hood (car)*
cappuccino (m) *cappuccino*
cápsula (f) *capsule*
capucha (f) *hood*
cara (f) *face*
caramelos (m pl) *candy*
caravana (f) *camper van*
cardenal (m) *bruise*
cargar *to load*
cargo (m) *charge*
carnaval (m) *carnival*
carne (f) *meat*
carné de conducir (m)
  driver's license
carné de estudiante (m)
  student card
carnicería (f) *butcher*
caro *expensive*
carrera (f) *run; race*
carrete (m) *roll (of film)*
carretera (f) *road*
carretera principal (f)
  main road
carreteras (f pl) *roads*
carril de bicicletas (m)
  cycle lane
carta (f) *letter; menu*
carta de vinos (f) *wine list*
cartas (f pl) *cards*

cartero/a (m/f) *letter carrier*
cartulina (f) *cardboard*
casa (f) *house; home*
casado *married*
casco de ciclista (m)
  cycle helmet
casi *almost*
casino (m) *casino*
castaño *brunette*
castillo (m) *castle*
catamarán (m) *catamaran*
catedral (f) *cathedral*
CD (m) *CD*
cebolla (f) *onion*
ceja (f) *eyebrow*
celebración (f) *celebration*
cena (f) *dinner; supper*
cenicero (m) *ashtray*
centro (m) *center*
centro comercial (m)
  shopping center
centro deportivo (m)
  sports center
cepillo (m) *brush; plane*
cerca *near*
cerca de *next to*
cerdo (m) *pork*
cereales (m pl)
  breakfast cereals
cerebro (m) *brain*
cereza (f) *cherry*
cerilla (f) *match (light)*
cero *zero*
cerrado *closed*
cerradura (f) *lock*
cerrar *to close*
cerrar sesión *to log out*
cerveza (f) *beer*
cesto (m) *basket*
chaleco salvavidas
  (m) *life jacket*
champán (m) *champagne*
champú (m) *shampoo*

chanclas (f pl) *flip-flop*
chaqueta (f) *jacket*
chaquetón (m) *parka*
charcutería (f) *delicatessen*
chef (m/f) *chef*
cheque (m) *check*
chicle (m) *chewing gum*
chico/a (m/f) *boy; girl*
chorizo (m) *chorizo*
chuleta (f) *chop*
cibercafé (m) *internet café*
cien *hundred*
cigarrillo (m) *cigarette*
cilantro (m) *cilantro*
cinco *five*
cine (m) *movie theater*
cinta adhesiva
  (f) *adhesive tape*
cinturón (m) *belt*
círculo (m) *circle*
ciruela (f) *plum*
cirujano/a (m/f) *surgeon*
cita (f) *appointment*
  (arrangement to meet)
cítricos (m pl) *citrus fruit*
citronela (f) *lemon grass*
ciudad (f) *city*
clase (f) *class; type*
clase preferente (f)
  business class
cláxon (m) *horn*
cliente/a (m/f) *customer*
clínica (f) *clinic*
club de jazz (m) *jazz club*
club nocturno (m) *nightclub*
cobrar *to charge*
cocer al horno *to bake*
coche (m) *car*
coche de cinco puertas (m)
  hatchback
coche patrulla (m) *police car*
cocina (f) *kitchen*
cocinar *to cook*

coco (m) *coconut*
cóctel (m) *cocktail*
codo (m) *elbow*
coger *to catch; to get*
coger prestado *to borrow*
cojín (m) *cushion*
cola (f) *glue*
colador (m) *colander*
colchón (m) *mattress*
colegio (m) *school*
coliflor (f) *cauliflower*
colina (f) *hill*
collar (m) *necklace*
color (m) *color*
colorete (m) *blush*
columpios (m pl) *swings*
combinación (f) *slip*
comedor (m) *dining room*
comer *to eat*
comer fuera *to eat out*
comida (f) *food; lunch; meal*
comida al aire libre (f) *picnic*
comida de avión (f) *in-flight meal*
comida para llevar (f) *carry out*
comida rápida (f) *fast food*
comisaría (f) *police station*
comisión bancaria
  (f) *bank charge*
commutador de luces (m)
  lights switch
como *as; like*
¿cómo? *how?*
compañía de seguros
  (f) *insurance company*
compartimento
  (m) *compartment*
compartimento portaequipajes
  (m) *overhead bin*
compra (f) *groceries*
comprar *to buy*
compresa (f) *sanitary napkin*
comunicando *engaged/busy*
con *with*

concierto (m) *concert*
condón (m) *condom*
conducir *to drive*
conductor/a (m/f) *driver*
conductor/a de autobús (m/f)
  bus driver
conejo (m) *rabbit*
conexión (f) *connection*
confundido *confused*
congelado *frozen*
conocer *to meet; to know*
consigna (f) *left luggage*
construir *to build*
cónsul (m/f) *consul*
consulado (m) *consulate*
consulta (f) *consultation*
consulta del médico (f)
  doctor's office
contar *to count*
contento *happy*
contestador automático (m)
  answering machine
contestar *to answer*
continente (m) *continent*
control de pasaportes (m)
  passport control
copa (f) *glass*
copa de vino (f) *wine glass*
copia (f) *print*
corazón (m) *core; heart*
corbata (f) *tie*
corcho (m) *cork;
  bulletin board*
cordel (m) *string*
cordero (m) *lamb*
correcto *right (correct)*
correo (m) *mail*
corriente (f) *flow; current*
corriente eléctrica
  (f) *power*
cortar *to cut*
cortaúñas (m) *nail clippers*
corte de luz (m) *power outages*

corteza (f) *crust*
corto *short*
coser *to sew*
costa (f) *coast*
costilla (f) *rib*
crema con filtro solar (f)
  sunscreen
crema para después del sol
  (f) *aftersun*
crema protectora total (f)
  sunblock
cremallera (f) *zipper*
crepes (m/f pl) *crêpes*
croissant (m) *croissant*
crudo *raw*
cuaderno (m) *notebook*
cuadrado (m) *square*
¿cuántos? *how many?*
cuarto (m) *room; quarter; fourth*
cuarto de baño (m) *bathroom*
cuarto de estar (m) *living room*
cuarto para cambiar a los bebés
  (m) *baby changing room*
cubiertos (m pl) *cutlery*
cubo (m) *pail; bucket*
cubo de la basura
  (m) *garbage can*
cubo para reciclar (m)
  recycling bin
cucaracha (f) *cockroach*
cuchara (f) *spoon*
cuchara de postre (f)
  dessertspoon
cucharilla de café
  (f) *teaspoon*
cuchillo (m) *knife*
cuello (m) *neck*
cuenco (m) *bowl*
cuenta (f) *check (bill); account*
cuenta bancaria (f)
  bank account
cuenta corriente (f)
  checking account

cuenta de ahorros (f)
  savings account
cuerda (f) *rope*
cuerpo (m) *body*
cueva (f) *cave*
cultura (f) *culture*
cumpleaños (m) *birthday*
cuna (f) *crib*
curry (m) *curry*

D

dar *to give*
dar marcha atrás
  to reverse
dato (m) *detail*
de *of; from*
de nuevo *again*
de vacaciones
  on vacation
debajo de *below*
deber *to owe*
débil *weak*
decir *to say; to tell*
declaración (f) *statement*
decorado (m) *set*
dedo (m) *finger*
dejar *to leave*
delantal (m) *apron*
delante de *in front of*
delantero centro (m)
  forward (soccer)
delfín (m) *dolphin*
delgado *thin*
delicioso *delicious*
delincuencia (f) *crime*
delito (m) *crime (criminal offense)*
dentífrico (m) *toothpaste*
dentista (m/f) *dentist*
dentro *inside*
dentro de *into*
denuncia (f) *report to the
  police; complaint*
departamento (m) *department*

dependiente/a (m/f)
  salesperson
depilación a la cera (f)
  wuxing
deporte (m) *sport*
deportes acuáticos
  (m pl) *watersports*
deportes de invierno
  (m pl) *winter sports*
depósito (m) *deposit*
derecha (f) *right (direction)*
derribo (m) *throw*
desayuno (m) *breakfast*
descubierto (m) *overdraft*
descuento (m) *reduction*
desde *from*
desembarcar *to disembark*
desierto (m) *desert*
desinfectante (m) *antiseptic*
desmayarse *to faint*
desodorante (m) *deodorant*
despacho (m) *office; study*
despegar *take off*
despertarse *to wake up*
después *after*
destino (m) *destination*
detergente (m) *detergent*
detergente en polvo (m) *powder*
detergente líquido (m) *liquid*
detestar *to hate*
detrás de *behind*
día (m) *day*
día festivo (m) *public holiday*
diabético *diabetic*
diarrea (f) *diarrhea*
dibujar *to draw*
dibujo (m) *drawing*
diccionario (m) *dictionary*
diciembre (m) *December*
diente (m) *tooth*
dientes (m pl) *teeth*
diésel *diesel*
diez *ten*

difícil *difficult*
dinero (m) *money*
dirección (f) *address*
dirección de email (f)
   email address
direcciones *directions*
director/a del banco (m/f)
   bank manager
discutir *to discuss*
disfrutar *to enjoy*
disminuir la velocidad
   to slow down
distancia (f) *distance*
distrito (m) *district*
divisas (f pl) *foreign currency*
divorciado *divorced*
documentación (f)
   papers (identity)
documento adjunto (m)
   attachment
documento de identidad (m) *ID*
dolor (m) *pain*
dolor de cabeza (m) *headache*
dolor de estómago (m)
   stomach ache
doloroso *painful*
domiciliación bancaria (f)
   automatic payment
domingo (m) *Sunday*
¿dónde? *where?*
dormitorio (m) *bedroom*
dos *two*
dosis (f) *dosage*
ducha (f) *shower*
dulce *sweet*
durante *during*
duro *hard*
DVD (m) *DVD*

E

echar *to pour*
edificio (m) *apartment building*
edredón (m) *comforter*

edulcorante artificial
   (m) *artificial sweetener*
efecto secundario
   (m) *side effect*
él *he*
electricidad (f) *electricity*
electricista (m/f) *electrician*
ella *she; her*
compañero/a (m/f) *partner*
radio digital (f) *digital radio*
ello *it*
ellos/as *they; them*
embajada (f) *embassy*
embarazada *pregnant*
embarcar *to board*
emigrar *to emigrate*
empeine (m) *bridge*
empezar *to start*
empresa (f) *company*
empuje *push*
en *on; at; in*
encantar *to care for*
encender *to light*
enchufe (m) *plug*
encinta *pregnant*
encontrar *to find*
enero (m) *January*
enfadado *angry*
enfermedad (f) *illness*
enfermedad cardíaca (f)
   heart condition
enfermero/a (m/f) *nurse*
enfermo *ill; sick*
enfrente de *opposite*
enjuague bucal
   (m) *mouthwash*
enrutador (m) *router*
ensalada (f) *salad*
ensayo (m) *try*
enseñanza superior (f) *college*
entero *whole*
entrada (f) *entrance;
   entrance ticket*

entrada familiar
   (f) *family ticket*
entrante (m) *appetizer*
entre *between*
entretenimiento (m)
   entertainment
entusiasmado *excited*
enviar *to send*
envuelto para regalo *gift-wrap*
epiléptico *epileptic*
equipaje (m) *luggage*
equipaje de mano (m)
   hand luggage
equipaje permitido (m)
   baggage allowance
equipamiento (m) *equipment*
equipo (m) *team; equipment*
equipo estéreo del coche
   (m) *car stereo*
error (m) *mistake*
escalada (f) *rock climbing*
escalera (f) *staircase*
escaleras (f pl) *stairs*
escáner (m) *scan*
escape (m) *leak*
escarabajo (m) *beetle*
escarcha (f) *frost*
escenario (m) *stage*
escoba (f) *broom*
escribir *to write*
escuchar *to listen*
ese/a *that*
esguince (m) *sprain*
espalda (f) *back (body)*
España *Spain*
español *Spanish*
espantoso *awful*
espátula (f) *spatula*
especias (f pl) *spices*
espejo (m) *mirror*
espina dorsal (f) *spine*
espinaca (f) *spinach*
esponja (f) *sponge*

esposas (f pl)
   handcuffs
espuma de afeitar (f)
   shaving foam
esquí (m) *ski*
esquí acuático
   (m) *waterskiing*
esquiar *to ski*
esquíes (m pl) *skis*
estación (f) *season; station*
estación de autobuses (f)
   bus station
estación del tren
   train station
estación de tren (f)
   train station
estante (m) *shelf*
estar *to be*
estatua (f) *statue*
este (m) *east*
éste/a *this*
estómago (m) *stomach*
estornudo (m) *sneeze*
estrecho *narrow*
estreñimiento (m)
   constipation
estrés (m) *stress*
estropeado *damaged*
estructura (f) *frame*
estudiante (m/f) *student*
etiqueta de identificación
   de equipaje (f) *baggage claim
   tag*
etiquetas (f pl) *labels*
euro (m) *euro*
exactamente *exactly*
examinar *to examine*
excursión (f) *excursion*
excursión en barco
   (f) *boat trip*
experiencia (f) *experience*
exposición (f) *exhibition*
expulsión (f) *send off*

extintor (m)
  fire extinguisher
extra *extra*
extreñimiento (m)
  constipation

F

fácil *easy*
facturar *to check in (at airport)*
falda (f) *skirt*
familia (f) *family*
farmacéutico/a (m/f) *pharmacist*
farmacia (f) *pharmacy*
faro (m) *headlight; lighthouse*
febrero (m) *February*
fecha de caducidad (f)
  sell-by date
feliz *happy*
feo *ugly*
ferretería (f)
  hardware store
ferrocarril (m) *railroad*
ferry (m) *ferry*
ficha (f) *counter*
fiebre (f) *fever*
fiebre del heno (f)
  hay fever
fiesta nacional (f)
  public holiday
fiestas (f pl) *festivals*
fila (f) *row*
filete (m) *steak*
final (m) *end*
firma (f) *signature*
firmar *to sign*
flash (m) *flash gun*
flores (f pl) *flowers*
florista (m/f) *florist*
flotador (m) *float*
folleto (m) *leaflet*
fontanero/a (m/f) *plumber*
footing (m) *jogging*
forma (f) *form*

forma física (f)
  fitness
fotocopiar
  to photocopy
fotografía (f) *photograph*
fotografía con flash (f)
  flash photography
fractura (f) *fracture*
frágil *fragile*
frambuesa (f)
  raspberry
franqueo (m) *postage*
frecuencia: con
  frecuencia *often*
fregar *to wash*
fregona (f) *mop*
freír *to fry*
freno (m) *brake*
fresa (f) *strawberry*
fresco *fresh*
friegaplatos (m)
  dishwasher
frigorífico (m)
  refrigerator
frigorífico congelador
  (m) *side-by-side refrigerator*
frío *cold*
frito *fried*
frito con mucho aceite
  deep-fried
frito con poco aceite
  pan fried
fritura (f) *stir-fry*
fruta (f) *fruit*
frutos secos (m pl) *nuts*
fuente (f) *fountain*
fuera *outside*
fuerte *strong*
fumar *to smoke*
funda (f) *case*
funda de la cámara (f)
  camera bag
fútbol (m) *soccer*

gachas de avena
 (f pl) *porridge*
gafas (f pl) *glasses*
gafas de buceo (f pl)
 diving mask
gafas de natación (f pl) *goggles*
gafas de sol (f pl) *sunglasses*
galería de arte (f) *art gallery*
galleta (f) *cookie*
gallinero (m) *balcony (in theater)*
gamba (f) *prawn*
ganar *to win*
garaje (m) *garage*
garantía (f) *guarantee*
garbanzos (m pl) *chickpeas*
gas (m) *gas*
gas con gas *sparkling*
gasolina (f) *gasoline*
gasolinera (f) *gas station*
gato (m) *cat*
gel de ducha (m)
 shower gel
gemelos (m pl) *cufflinks*
gimnasio (m) *gym*
ginebra (f) *gin*
glorieta (f) *traffic circle*
golf (m) *golf*
gorro de baño (m) *bathing cap;*
 swimming cap
grabado (m) *engraving*
gracias (f pl) *thanks*
grados (m pl) *degrees*
gráfica del paciente
 (f) *chart*
gramo (m) *gram*
Gran Bretaña *Great Britain*
granada (f) *pomegranate*
grande *big; large*
grandes almacenes (m pl)
 department store
granizo (m) *hail*
granja (f) *farm*

granjero/a (m/f) *farmer*
granos (m pl) *beans*
grasa (f) *fat*
gratis *free (no charge)*
grave *serious*
grifo (m) *faucet*
gripe (f) *flu*
gris *gray*
gritar *to shout*
grosella negra (f)
 blackcurrant
grueso *thick*
grupo (m) *group*
guante de béisbol (m)
 baseball glove
guantes (m pl) *gloves*
guapo *handsome*
guardacostas
 (m) *coast guard*
guarnición (f) *side dish*
guía (f) *guide; guidebook*
guía en audio (f)
 audio guide
guindilla (f) *chili*
guiso (m) *stew*
gustar *to like*

H

habitación (f) *room*
habitación con desayuno incluido
 (f) *bed and breakfast*
habitación con dos camas
 individuales (f) *room with two*
 twin beds
habitación doble (f)
 double room
habitación familiar (f)
 family room
habitación individual (f)
 single room
hablar *to speak;*
 to talk
hacer *to do; to make*

hacer de canguro
babysitting
hacer fotos *to take photos*
hacer la maleta *to pack*
hacer surf *to surf*
hacia *towards*
hamaca (f) *deck chair*
hamburguesa (f) *burger*
hamburguesa vegetariana
(f) *veggie burger*
hasta *until*
hay *there is/there are*
hebilla (f) *buckle*
helada (f) *freeze*
hemorragia (f) *bleeding*
hemorragia nasal
(f) *nosebleed*
herida (f) *wound; injury*
herir *to injure*
hermano/a (m/f) *brother, sister*
hermoso *beautiful*
hervido *boiled*
hervidor de agua (m) *kettle*
hervidor de agua para camping
(m) *camping kettle*
hervir *to boil*
hielo (m) *ice*
hierba (f) *herb*
hígado (m) *liver*
hijo/a (m/f) *son, daughter*
hipódromo (m)
racecourse
hockey (m) *hockey*
hogar (m) *home*
hola *hello*
hombre (m) *man*
hombro (m) *shoulder*
hora (f) *hour*
hora de dormir (f)
bed time
horario (m) *timetable*
horario de apertura (m)
opening hours

horario de visitas (m)
visiting hours
hornillo para camping (m)
camping stove
horno (m) *oven*
hospital (m) *hospital*
hotel (m) *hotel*
huésped (m) *guest*
húmedo *humid*
humo (m) *smoke*
huracán (m) *hurricane*

I

iglesia (f) *church*
imprimir *to print*
impuestos (m pl) *taxes*
incendio (m) *fire*
indicador del nivel
de la gasolina (m) *fuel gauge*
infección (f) *infection*
informar de *to report*
inglés *English*
ingresar *to deposit (bank)*
inhalador (m) *inhaler*
iniciar sesión *to log on*
inmigración *immigration*
interesante *interesting*
interesar *to interest*
interior: del interior
inland
intérprete (m)
interpreter
interruptor (m) *switch*
inundación (f) *flood*
inventario (m) *inventory*
investigación (f) *research*
invierno (m) *winter*
invitado (m) *guest*
inyección (f) *injection*
iPod (m) *iPod*
ir *to go*
ir de compras
to go shopping

ir de discotecas
 to go clubbing
ir en bicicleta *to cycle*
isla (f) *island*
izquierda (f) *left (direction)*

J

jabón (m) *soap*
jaqueca (f) *migraine*
jarabe para la tos (m)
 cough syrup
jardín (m) *garden*
jarra (f) *pitchers*
jefe/a (m/f) *manager*
jengibre (m) *ginger*
jersey (m) *sweater*
jirafa (f) *giraffe*
joven *young*
joyas (f pl) *jewelry*
joyería (f) *jewelry store*
jubilado *retired*
juego (m) *game*
jugar *to play (games)*
julio (m) *July*
junco (m) *rush*
junio (m) *June*

K

kilagramo (m) *kilogram*
kilómetro (m) *kilometer*

L

lácteos (m pl) *dairy*
ladera (f) *slope*
lado (m) *side*
lado: al lado de
 beside
ladrillo (m) *brick*
lago (m) *lake*
lana (f) *wool*
lápiz (m) *pencil*
lápiz de colores (m)
 colored pencil

lápiz de ojos
 (m) *eyeliner*
largo *long*
lata (f) *can (noun)*
lavabo (m) *sink*
lavadero de coches (m)
 car wash
lavadora (f)
 washing machine
lavandería (f)
 laundromat
leche (f) *milk*
lechuga (f) *lettuce*
leer *to read*
lejía (f) *bleach*
lejos *far*
lengua (f) *tongue*
lente (f) *lens*
lentes de contacto (f pl)
 contact lenses
lento *slow*
lesión (f) *injury*
lesionar *to injure*
letrero (m) *sign*
levar *to prove (baking)*
libra (f) *sterling; pound*
libre *free (not engaged)*
librería (f) *bookstore*
libro (m) *book*
licuadora (f) *blender*
ligero *light (not heavy)*
limonada (f) *lemonade*
limón (m) *lemon*
limpiador/a (m/f) *cleaner*
limpio *clean*
línea del bateador (f) *crease*
lista (f) *list*
lista de precios (f) *price list*
lista de vinos (f) *wine list*
listo *ready*
litera (f) *sleeper berths*
litro (m) *liter*
llamada (f) *phone call*

llave (f) *key*
llave de la habitación (f)
 room key
llave de paso (f) *water valve*
llave USB (f) *memory stick*
llegadas (f pl) *arrivals*
llegar *to arrive*
llenar *to fill*
lleno *full*
llevar *to take;*
 to carry; to wear
llorar *to cry*
lloviendo *raining*
loción corporal (f) *body lotion*
lo/la *it*
loncha (f) *slice*
longitud (f) *length*
luces (f pl) *lights*
luces antiniebla (f pl)
 hazard lights
lugar (m) *place*
lugares de interés (m pl)
 attractions
lunar (m) *mole (medical)*
lunes (m) *Monday*
luz (f) *light*

M

machacado *crushed*
madre (f) *mother*
maduro *ripe*
maíz (m) *corn*
maleta (f) *suitcase*
maletero (m) *trunk (car)*
maletín (m) *briefcase*
malo *bad*
mañana *tomorrow*
mañana (f) *morning*
mancha (f) *pump (bicycle)*
mandar *to send*
mandíbula (f) *jaw*
mando a distancia (m)
 remote control

mango (m) *mango*
manguito (m) *water wings*
 manicura (f) *manicure*
manilla (f) *handle*
mano (f) *hand*
manoplas para el horno
 (f pl) *oven mitts*
manta (f) *blanket*
mantener *to keep; to maintain*
mantequilla (f) *butter*
mantequilla de cacahuetes
 (f) *peanut butter*
manual *manual*
manuscrito (m) *manuscript*
manzana (f) *apple*
mapa (m) *map*
maquillaje (m) *makeup*
máquina (f) *machine*
máquina de billetes (f)
 automatic ticket machine
máquina de café (f)
 coffee machine
máquina de remo (f)
 rowing machine
maquinilla de afeitar
 (f) *razor*
maquinilla eléctrica (f)
 electric razor
mar (m) *sea*
marcar *to dial*
marco para fotos (m)
 photo frame
marido (m) *husband*
marisco (m) *seafood*
marrón *brown*
marzo (m) *March*
más *more*
más allá de *beyond*
más o menos *about*
masaje (m) *massage*
matrícula (f) *number plate;*
 registration number
mayo (m) *May*

mayonesa (f) *mayonnaise*
mazo (m) *mallet*
mecánico/a (m/f) *mechanic*
mechero (m) *lighter*
medianoche (f) *midnight*
medicina (f) *medicine*
médico/a (m/f) *doctor*
medida (f) *measure*
medio *half*
mediodía (m) *noon*
medusa (f) *jellyfish*
mejilla (f) *cheek*
mejor *better*
mensaje (m) *message*
mensaje de texto (SMS)
 (m) *text*
mensaje de voz (m)
 voice message
mensajero/a (m/f) *courier*
mensajes (m pl) *messages*
menta (f) *mint*
menú (m) *menu*
menú de la cena (m)
 evening menu
menú de la comida (m)
 lunch menu
mercado (m) *market*
mermelada (f) *jam*
mermelada de naranja (f)
 marmalade
mes (m) *month*
mesa (f) *table*
mesa de café (f)
 coffee table
metal (m) *metal*
metro (m) *meter;*
 subway
mi *my*
microondas (m)
 microwave
milla (f) *mile*
minibar (m) *mini bar*
minuto (m) *minute*

mirar *to watch*
mismo *same*
mitad (f) *half*
mixto *mixed*
mochila (f) *backpack*
moda (f) *fashion*
modo de empleo
 (m) *instructions*
modalidades (f pl) *events*
molido *ground*
moneda (f) *coin*
monedero (m) *change purse*
mono (m) *monkey*
montaña (f) *mountain*
montar a caballo
 to go horseback riding
montar una tienda
 to pitch a tent
monumento (m) *monument*
moqueta (f) *carpet*
mora (f) *blackberry*
morado *purple*
mordisco (m) *bite*
moreno *dark*
mosquitera (f) *mosquito net*
mosquito (m) *mosquito*
mostaza (f) *mustard*
mostrador (m) *desk*
mostrador de facturación (m)
 check-in desk
moto (f) *motorcycle*
moto acuática (f) *jet ski*
motor (m) *engine*
móvil (m) *cell phone*
mucho *much*
muchos *many*
mujer (f) *woman; female*
mujer policía (f)
 policewoman
multa (f) *fine (legal)*
muñeca (f) *doll*
músculos (m pl) *muscles*
museo (m) *museum*

música (f) *music*
música de baile (f) *dance*
músico/a (m/f) *musician*

N

nacimiento (m) *birth*
nada *nothing*
nadar *to swim*
naranja (f) *orange*
nariz (f) *nose*
natación (f) *swimming*
nata (f) *cream*
naúsea (f) *nausea*
navegador por satélite (m) *GPS receiver*
navegar *to sail*
necesitar *to need*
negocio (m) *business*
negro *black*
nervioso *nervous*
neumático (m) *tire*
nevera (f) *cooler*
niebla (f) *misty; fog*
nieve (f) *snow*
niño/a (m/f) *child*
no *no; not*
noche (f) *evening; night*
nombre (m) *name*
normal *normal*
norte (m) *north*
nota (f) *bill; note*
noticia (f) *news*
noviembre (m) *November*
novio/a (m/f) *boy/girlfriend*
nube (f) *cloud*
nublado *cloudy*
nuestro *our*
nueve *nine*
nuevo *new*
número (m) *number; size (shoes)*
número de contacto (m) *contact number*

número de la cuenta (m) *account number*
número de vuelo (m) *flight number*
nunca *never*

O

o *or*
objetos perdidos (m pl) *lost property*
obra (f) *construction site*
obra de teatro (f) *play*
obras (f pl) *roadwork*
océano (m) *ocean*
ocio (m) *leisure*
octubre (m) *October*
ocupado *occupied*
oficina (f) *office*
oficina de cambio (f) *currency exchange*
oficina de correos (f) *post office*
oficina de información (f) *tourist information*
oír *to hear*
ojo (m) *eye*
ola (f) *wave*
olla (f) *casserole dish*
olvidar *to forget*
operación (f) *operation*
ópera (f) *opera*
orador/a (m/f) *speaker*
ordenador (m) *computer*
oreja (f) *ear*
orgulloso *proud*
oro (m) *gold*
oso/a (m/f) *bear*
otoño (m) *fall*
otra vez *again*
otro *another; other*
ovillo (m) *ball*
óvulo (m) *egg*

paciente (m/f) *patient*
padre (m) *father*
padres (m pl) *parents*
pagar *to pay*
pago (m) *payment*
país (m) *country*
palo de golf (m) *golf club*
pan (m) *bread*
pan moreno (m)
whole-wheat bread
pan tostado (m) *toast*
panadería (f) *baker*
pañal (m) *diaper*
panecillo (m) *bread roll*
pantalones (m pl) *pants*
**pantalones cortos
(m pl)** *shorts*
panti (m) *panty hose*
pantuflas (f pl) *slippers*
pañuelo de papel (m)
tissue
papel (m) *paper*
papelera (f) *trash*
papeles (m pl)
papers (identity)
paquete (m) *package, packet*
par (m) *pair*
para *for*
para comer en el local *eat-in*
para llevar *take-away*
parabólica (f) *satellite dish*
parachoques (m) *bumper*
parada (f) *block (soccer)*
**parada de autobús
(f)** *bus stop*
**parada de taxis
(f)** *taxi stand*
parar *to stop; to save (soccer)*
pareja (f) *couple*
parientes (m pl) *relatives*
parmesano (m) *parmesan*
parque (m) *park*

parque de atracciones (m)
fairground
parque nacional (m)
national park
parquímetro (m) *parking meter*
partida de nacimiento (f)
birth certificate
partido (m) *match (sport)*
partitura (f) *score*
parto (m) *delivery (childbirth)*
pasajero/a (m/f) *passenger*
pasaporte (m) *passport*
pasar *to happen*
pasar la bayeta *to wipe*
pasatiempos (m pl)
leisure activities
pase (m) *pass*
**pase para el telesilla
(m)** *lift pass*
paseo (m) *trekking*
pasillo (m) *aisle*
paso (m) *walk; step*
paso de peatones (m)
pedestrian crossing
paso de zebra (m)
zebra crossing
paso subterráneo (m)
underpass
pasta (f) *pasta*
pastel (m) *cake; pastry; pie*
pastilla (f) *pill; tablet*
pastilla para la garganta (f)
throat lozenge
patata (f) *potato*
patatas fritas (f pl) *potato chips*
patín (m) *skate*
patinaje sobre hielo (m)
ice-skating
patio (m) *courtyard*
patio de butacas (m) *stalls*
pato (m) *duck*
pausa (f) *rest; pause*
peaje (m) *toll*

peces (m pl) *fish*
pecho (m) *chest*
pedicura (f) *pedicure*
pedir *to order*
peine (m) *comb*
pelador (m) *peeler*
pelar *to peel*
película (f) *movie*
peligro (m) *danger*
pelo (m) *hair*
pelota (f) *ball*
pelota de golf (f) *golf ball*
pelota de playa (f) *beach ball*
pelota de tenis (f) *tennis ball*
peluche (m) *stuffed animal*
peluquería (f) *hairdresser's*
pendiente (m) *earring*
pensar *to think*
pensión (f) *guesthouse*
pensionista (m/f) *senior citizen*
peor *worse*
pepino (m) *cucumber*
pequeño *small*
pera (f) *pear*
percha (f) *coat hanger*
perder *to lose; to miss*
perdone *excuse me*
perejil (m) *parsley*
perfume (m) *perfume*
periferia (f) *suburb*
periódico (m) *newspaper*
pero *but*
perro/a (m/f) *dog*
persona (f) *person*
persona minusválida (f)
   disabled person
personal (m) *staff*
personas (f pl) *people*
pesado *heavy*
pesa (f) *weight*
pesar *to weigh*
pescadería (f)
   fish seller

pescar *fishing*
pestaña (f) *eyelash*
pianista (m/f) *pianist*
picante *spicy*
pie (m) *foot*
piedra preciosa (f) *gemstone*
piel (f) *skin*
pierna (f) *leg*
pijama (m) *pyjamas*
pila (f) *battery*
píldoras para el mareo
   (f pl) *travel-sickness pills*
piloto (m/f) *pilot*
pimienta (f) *pepper*
pin (m) *PIN*
piña (f) *pineapple*
pinchazo (m) *flat tire*
pinta (f) *pint*
pintor/a (m/f) *painter; artist*
pintura (f) *painting*
pinzas (f pl) *tweezers*
piqueta (f) *tent peg*
piscina descubierta (f)
   outdoor pool
piscina (f) *swimming pool*
pista de esquí (f) *ski slope*
pista de tenis (f) *tennis court*
pista para principiantes
   (f) *green slope*
pizza (f) *pizza*
plancha (f) *griddle pan; iron*
planeta (m) *planet*
plano (m) *street map*
plano del metro (m)
   subway map
plantas (f pl) *plants*
plata (f) *silver*
plátano (m) *banana*
platillo (m) *saucer*
plato (m) *dish; plate*
plato principal (m)
   main course
platos (m pl) *courses*

platos del día
  (m pl) *specials*
playa (f) *beach*
plaza (f) *square (in town)*
poco *a little*
poder *can (verb)*
policía (f) *police*
policía (m/f) *police officer*
póliza (f) *policy*
póliza de seguros (f)
  insurance policy
pollo (m) *chicken*
pomada (f) *ointment*
poner *to put*
poner a remojo *to soak*
por *over; along*
por allí *over there*
por aquí cerca *nearby*
por avión *airmail*
por debajo de *beneath*
por favor *please*
por separado *separately*
por taequlpajes (m)
  luggage rack
portátil (m) *laptop*
posavasos (m) *coaster*
posible *possible*
postal (f) *postcard*
poste (m) *gate*
postre (m) *dessert*
precaución *caution*
precio (m) *price*
preferido *favorite*
preferir *to prefer*
prensa (f) *press*
preocupado *worried*
préstamo (m) *loan*
primavera (f) *spring*
primera planta (f)
  second floor
primero *first*
primeros auxilios (m pl)
  first aid

primo/a (m/f) *cousin*
principiante (m/f)
  beginner
principio (m) *beginning*
probador (m)
  fitting room
profesión (f) *occupation*
programa (m) *programme*
prohibida la entrada
  no entry
pronto *soon*
provincia (f) *province*
próximo *next*
prueba del embarazo (f)
  pregnancy test
público (m) *audience*
puerta (f) *door; gate*
puerta de embarque (f)
  boarding gate
puerta principal (f)
  front door
puerto deportivo (m)
  marina
puerto (m) *harbor*
puesta de sol (f) *sunset*
pulgada (f) *inch*
pulpo (m) *octopus*
pulsera (f) *bracelet*
punta (f) *tip*
punto (m) *point*
puro (m) *cigar*

Q

que *than*
quedarse *to stay*
quejarse *to complain*
quemadura (f) *burn*
quemadura del sol
  (f) *sunburn*
queso (m) *cheese*
queso cremoso (m)
  cream cheese
quince *fifteen*

quince días *fortnight*
quitarse *to take off (clothes)*
quizás *perhaps; maybe*

R

ración (f) *portion*
radiador (m) *radiator*
radio (f) *radio*
radio (m) *spoke*
radio despertador (f)
  clock radio
raíl (m) *rail*
raíz (f) *root*
rallador (m) *grater*
rama (f) *branch*
ramo (m) *bunch*
rápido *fast; quick*
raqueta de tenis (f)
  tennis racket
rara vez *rarely*
rasguño (m) *graze*
rata (f) *rat*
ratón (m) *mouse*
rebeca (f) *cardigan*
recepción (f) *reception*
recepcionista (m/f) *receptionist*
receta (f) *prescription*
recibir *to receive*
recibo (m) *receipt*
recipiente (m) *container*
recogedor (m) *dust pan*
recogida (f) *collection*
recogida de equipajes (f)
  baggage claim
recomendar *to recommend*
récord (m) *record*
recorrido guiado
  (m) *guided tour*
recto *straight*
recuerdo (m) *souvenir*
red (f) *net*
redondo *round*
refrescos (m pl) *soft drinks*

regalo (m) *gift; present*
región (f) *region*
registrarse *to check in*
reiniciar *to reboot*
reír *to laugh*
reloj (m) *clock; watch*
reloj despertador (m) *alarm clock*
remo (m) *oar*
remolacha (f) *beet*
remover *to stir*
reparación (f) *repair*
repelente de insectos (m)
  insect repellent
reposacabezas (m)
  head rest
representar *play (theater)*
reproductor de DVD (m)
  DVD player
reserva (f) *reservation*
reservar *to book; to reserve*
reservar un vuelo *to book a flight*
resfriado (m) *cold (illness)*
respaldo (m) *back (chair)*
restaurante (m) *restaurant*
resto (m) *return*
retraso: con retraso *delayed*
revelar *to develop (a film)*
revisión (f) *checkup*
revisor (m) *ticket inspector*
revista (f) *magazine*
rímel (m) *mascara*
río (m) *river*
rizado *curly*
robado *stolen*
robar *to burgle*
roca (f) *rock*
rodaja (f) *slice*
rodilla (f) *knee*
rodilleras (f pl) *pads*
rojo *red*
rollo de papel higiénico
  (m) *toilet papers*
rompiente (f) *surf*

roncar *to snore*
ropa (f) *clothes*
ropa de cama (f) *bed linen*
ropa interior (f) *underwear*
rosa *pink*
rosquilla (f) *bagel*
rubí (m) *ruby*
rubio *blonde*
rueda de repuesto (f)
  spare tire
ruidoso *noisy*

S

sábado (m) *Saturday*
sábana bajera (f) *sheet*
saber *to know (a fact)*
sacacorchos (m)
  corkscrew
saco de dormir (m)
  sleeping bag
safari (m) *safari park*
sal (f) *salt*
sala de embarque (f)
  departure lounge
sala de la estación (f)
  concourse
sala de urgencias (f)
  emergency room
salado *salted; savory*
salami (m) *salami*
salchicha (f) *sausage*
salida (f) *exit*
salida de emergencia (f)
  emergency exit
salida de incendios (f)
  fire escape
salidas (f pl) *departures*
salir *to go out*
salmón (m) *salmon*
salpicadero (m) *dashboard*
salsa (f) *sauce*
saltar *to dive*
saltear *to sauté*

salud *cheers*
salud (f) *health*
salvavidas (m) *life ring*
sandalia (f) *sandal*
sandía (f) *watermelon*
sarpullido (m) *rash*
sartén (f) *frying pan*
sastre/a (m/f) *tailor*
sauna (f) *sauna*
secadora (f) *tumble dryer*
secador de pelo (m)
  blow-dryer
secar con el secador
  to blow dry
seco *dry*
seda (f) *silk*
segunda planta (f)
  third floor
segundo *second (position)*
seguridad (f) *security*
seguro *safe*
seguro (m) *insurance*
seguro de sí mismo *confident*
seguro médico (m)
  health insurance
sello (m) *stamp*
selva tropical (f) *rain forest*
semáforo (m) *traffic light*
semana pasada (f)
  last week
semana que viene (f)
  next week
semilla (f) *seed*
señal (f) *signal*
señal de tráfico
  (f) *road sign*
señalizar *signpost*
senderismo (m) *hiking*
sendero (m) *footpath*
sensible *sensitive*
sentarse *to sit*
sentencia (f) *sentence*
sentir *to feel*

septiembre (m)
  September
ser *to be*
serpiente (f) *snake*
servicio (m) *serve*
servicio rápido (m)
  express service
servicios (m pl)
  services
servicios de urgencia (m pl)
  emergency services
servilleta (f)
  napkin
servir *to serve*
seta (f) *mushroom*
siempre *always*
siento: lo siento
  I'm sorry
silla (f) *chair*
silla de ruedas (f)
  wheelchair
simpático *nice (person)*
sin pepitas *seedless*
sirena (f) *siren*
snowboarding (m)
  snowboarding
sobre *above; onto*
sobre (m) *envelope*
socorrista (m/f)
  lifeguard
soda (f)
  soda water
sofá (m) *sofa*
sofá-cama (m)
  sofa bed
sol (m) *sun;*
  sunshine
solo *alone*
sólo *only*
soltar *to release*
soltero *single*
  (not married)
sombrero (m) *sunhat*

sombrilla (f)
  beach umbrella
somnífero (m)
  sleeping pill
sonrisa (f) *smile*
sopa (f) *soup*
soporte (m) *rack;*
  stand; support
sorbete (m)
  sherbet
sorprendido
  surprised
sostenido *sharp (music)*
sótano (m)
  basement
sport *casual (clothing)*
stepper (m)
  step machine
su *his/her/its/their/your*
suavizante (m)
  conditioner
sucio *dirty*
sudadera (f)
  sweatshirt
suelo (m) *floor*
sujetar *to hold*
sumar *to add*
sumidero (m) *drain*
supermercado (m)
  supermarket
supositorios (m pl)
  suppositories
sur (m) *south*

T

tabaco (m)
  tobacco
tabla de cortar (f)
  cutting board
tabla de planchar (f)
  ironing board
tabla de snowboard (f)
  snowboard

tabla de surf (f)
  surfboard
tablero de anuncios de salidas
  (m) *departure board*
tablilla (f) *splint*
talla (f) *size (clothes)*
talón (m) *heel (body)*
talonario de cheques (m)
  checkbook
también *too (also)*
tampón (m) *tampon*
tan *so*
tanque (m) *tank*
tapa (f) *lid*
taquilla (f)
  box office
taquillas (f pl)
  lockers
tarde *late*
tarde (f)
  afternoon
tarifa (f) *fare*
tarjeta (f) *card*
tarjeta bancaria (f)
  check card
tarjeta de crédito (f)
  credit card
tarjeta de débito(f)
  debit card
tarjeta de embarque (f)
  boarding pass
tarjeta de memoria (f)
  memory card
tarjeta telefónica (f)
  phone card
tarrina (f) *tub*
tarro (m) *jar*
taxi (m) *taxi*
taxista (m/f)
  taxi driver
taza (f) *cup*
taza de café (f)
  coffee cup

té (m) *tea*
té negro (m)
  black tea
té verde (m)
  green tea
teatro de la ópera (m)
  opera house
tebeo (m)
  comic book
techo (m) *ceiling; roof*
teclado (m)
  keyboard
tee de golf (m)
  golf tee
tejanos (m pl)
  jeans
tela (f) *fabric*
teleférico (m)
  cable car
teléfono (m)
  telephone
teléfono inteligente (m)
  smartphone
teléfono público (m)
  payphone
telesilla (m)
  chair lift
televisión (f)
  television
televisión por cable (f)
  cable television
televisión por satélite (f)
  satellite TV
televisor (m)
  television set
telón (m) *curtain*
temperatura (f)
  temperature
temprano *early*
tenedor (m)
  fork
tener *to have*
tenis (m) *tennis*

tensión alta (f)
high blood pressure
tensión arterial (f)
blood pressure
tentempié (m) *snack*
terminal (f) *terminal*
terminar *to finish*
termómetro (m)
thermometer
ternera (f) *beef*
terremoto (m) *earthquake*
tetera (f) *teapot*
tetrabrik (m) *carton*
tía (f) *aunt*
tiburón (m) *shark*
tienda (f) *store; shop; tent*
tienda de artículos de regalo
(f) *gift store*
tienda de discos (f)
record store
tienda de muebles (f)
furniture store
tienda libre de impuestos (f)
duty-free store
tierra (f) *soil*
tijeras (f pl) *scissors*
tijeras para las uñas (f pl)
nail scissors
tilo (m) *lime tree*
timbre (m)
bell; call button
tímido *shy*
tío (m) *uncle*
tirante (m) *strap*
tirarse *to dive*
tirita (f) *adhesive bandage*
toalla de baño (f)
bath towel
toalla de playa (f)
beach towel
toallas (f pl) *towels*
toallita húmeda (f)
wet wipe

tobillo (m) *ankle*
tobogán (m) *slide*
todo *all*
todo recto
straight on
toga (f) *robe*
tomar el sol
to sunbathe
tomate (m) *tomato*
tomate cherry (m)
cherry tomato
tormenta: hay tormenta
stormy; it's stormy
tornear *to turn*
tortilla (f) *omelet*
tos (f) *cough*
tostador (m) *toaster*
trabajo (m) *work*
tráfico (m) *traffic*
traje (m) *suit*
traje de buzo
(m) *wetsuit*
traje de noche (m)
evening dress
tranquilo *calm*
transferencia bancaria (f)
bank transfer
transporte (m)
transportations
tranvía (m) *tram*
trasero (m) *bottom (body)*
trébol (m) *club*
treinta *thirty*
tren de alta velocidad (m)
high-speed train
tres *three*
trigo (m) *wheat*
trípode (m) *tripod*
triste *upset; sad*
trona (f) *high chair*
trozo de (m) *piece*
trucha (f) *trout*
tubo (m) *tube*

tubo de buceo
  (m) *snorkel*
tubo de escape (m)
  exhaust (car)
tumbona (f)
  lounge chair
turismo (m)
  sightseeing; sedan (car)
turista (m) *tourist*
turno (m) *move*

U

último *last*
un/una *a*
uña (f) *nail*
unidad de cuidados intensivos
  (f) *intensive care unit*
uniforme (m) *uniform*
universidad (f) *university*
uno/una *one*
unos *some*
un poco *a little*
urgencia (f)
  emergency
urgencias (f pl) *accident*
  and emergency department

V

vaca (f) *cow/beef*
vacaciones (f pl) *vacation*
vacío *empty*
vagón comedor (m)
  dining car
vagón restaurante (m)
  dining car
vajilla (f) *dishes*
vale *ok*
válido *valid*
valla (f) *fence*
valor (m) *value*
vapor: al vapor *steamed*
vaso (m) *glass*
veces: a veces *sometimes*

vegeteriano *vegetarian*
veinte *twenty*
vela (f) *sailing*
velocidad máxima (f)
  speed limit
velocímetro (m)
  speedometer
vendaje (m) *bandage*
vender *to sell*
venir *to come*
ventana (f) *window*
ventilador (m) *fan*
ver *to see*
verano (m) *summer*
verde *green*
verdulería (f)
  greengrocery
verdura (f) *vegetables*
vespa (f) *scooter*
vestíbulo de llegadas (m)
  arrivals hall
vestíbulo de salidas (m)
  departures hall
vestido (m) *dress*
veterinaria (f) *vet*
vía (f) *track*
vía de acceso (f)
  entrance ramp
viajar *to travel*
viejo *old*
viernes (m) *Friday*
vinagre (m) *vinegar*
violación (f) *rape*
virus (m) *virus*
vista (f) *vision*
vitaminas (f pl)
  vitamins
volante (m)
  steering wheel
volar *to fly*
volumen (m) *volume*
vomitar *to vomit*
vuelo (m) *flight*

W

whisky (m) *whiskey*
Wi-Fi (f) *wifi*

Y

y *and*
ya *already*
yate (m) *yacht*
yo *I (1st person)*
yo mismo *myself*
yogur (m) *yogurt*

Z

zanahoria (f) *carrot*
zapatería (f) *shoe store*
zapato (m) *shoe*

zona (f) *zone*
zona de fumadores
  smoking area
zoológico (m) *zoo*
zumo (m) *juice*
zumo de manzana (m)
  apple juice
zumo de naranja (m)
  orange juice

ACKNOWLEDGMENTS

ORIGINAL EDITION

Senior Editors Simon Tuite, Angela Wilkes
Editorial Assistant Megan Jones
US Editor Margaret Parrish
Senior Art Editor Vicky Short
Art Editor Mandy Earey
Production Editor Phil Sergeant
Production Controller Inderjit Bhullar
Managing Editor Julie Oughton
Managing Art Editor Louise Dick
Art Director Bryn Walls
Associate Publisher Liz Wheeler
Publisher Jonathan Metcalf

Produced for Dorling Kindersley by
SP Creative Design
Editor Heather Thomas
Designer Rolando Ugolino
Language content for Dorling
Kindersley by
First Edition Translations Ltd
Translator Elena Urena
Typesetting Essential Typesetting

Dorling Kindersley would also like to thank the following for their help in
the preparation of the original and revised editions of this book: Isabelle Elkaim
and Melanie Fitzgerald of First Edition Translations Ltd; Lima Aquino, Mandy
Earey, and Meenal Goel for design assistance; Amelia Collins, Nicola Hodgson,
Isha Sharma, Janashree Singha, Nishtha Kapil, and Neha Ruth Samuel for
editorial assistance; Claire Bowers, Lucy Claxton, and Rose Horridge in the
DK Picture Library; Adam Brackenbury, Vânia Cunha, Almudena Diaz,
Maria Elia, John Goldsmid, Sonia Pali, Phil Sergeant, and Louise Waller
for DTP assistance.

PICTURE CREDITS

EYEWITNESS TRAVEL

ILLUSTRATED THROUGHOUT AND NOW WITH FREE AUDIO

Organized by subject: everyday phrases, transportation, shopping, hotels, and more

•

Extensive menu guide and mini-dictionary

•

Free app offers audio of native speakers and key phrases, to perfect your pronunciation

Also from DK

www.dk.com

$7.95 USA / $9.95 Canada

ISBN 978-1-4654-6281-7 Printed in China

Download on the
App Store

GET IT ON
Google Play

5 0 7 9 5

9 781465 462817

ESSENTIAL REFERENCE FOR EVERY TRAVELER